A Genre for the Gospels

PHILIP L. SHULER

A Genre for the Gospels

The Biographical Character
of Matthew

FORTRESS PRESS   PHILADELPHIA

Library of Congress Cataloging in Publication Data

Shuler, Philip L.
  A genre for the Gospels.

  Bibliography: p.
  Includes index.
  1. Bible. N.T. Gospels—Criticism, interpretation, etc. 2. Bible. N.T. Matthew—Criticism, interpretation, etc. I. Title.
  BS2555.2.S47   226'066   81–71384
  ISBN 0–8006–0677–9   AACR2

9409L81   Printed in the United States of America 1–677

To:
MARGIE
Joel, Lance, and Suzanne

Contents

Abbreviations

AJT	*American Journal of Theology*
CBQ	*Catholic Biblical Quarterly*
HTR	*Harvard Theological Review*
Inst.	*Institutio oratoria.* Quintilian
JAAR	*Journal of the American Academy of Religion*
JBL	*Journal of Biblical Literature*
LCL	Loeb Classical Library
Rh.	*Rhetorica (The "Art" of Rhetoric).* Aristotle
Rh. Al.	*Rhetorica ad Alexandrinum.* Aristotle
SBL	Society of Biblical Literature
TR	*Theologische Rundschau*
USQR	*Union Seminary Quarterly Review*

Preface

My interest in the question of the genre of the gospels began in 1964 when I undertook to examine the possibility of making comparisons between Plutarch's *Lives* and the synoptic gospels by employing the rhetorical rules for the encomium as set forth by Hermogenes (second century A.D.). The idea for this project was precipitated by a mere reference in D. L. Clark's *Rhetoric in Greco-Roman Education*, namely, that the rhetorical device known as "comparison" (closely associated with the encomium) might possibly provide the key to the format of Plutarch's parallel lives. As I now reflect upon this task some twenty years later, I can still remember the difficulty I had trying to understand the results of the project in the context of the *sui generis* view of the gospels which then prevailed.

During the ensuing years, I have returned to various aspects of the question of gospel genre as time permitted. The present work represents the culmination of this research. Portions of the solution offered in this book were originally subjects of papers read at both national and regional meetings of the Society of Biblical Literature (Toronto in 1969 and 1974, New Orleans in 1971 and 1978, and St. Louis in 1975). These parts, however, were not combined into the present thesis until I was able to pursue graduate studies at McMaster University beginning in 1972. The thesis of the present work was first presented in the dissertation which was successfully defended at McMaster in 1975. This dissertation included discussions of each of the synoptic gospels.

The research has since been reexamined and rewritten. The scope has been limited to a consideration of the problems associated with identifying a genre with which the gospels may be related and an examination of the possible relationship of Matthew's gospel to the

genre that is identified. Thus the design of the present book is apparent: a general statement of problem and solution followed by a consideration of those generic conventions shared by Matthew's gospel.

It is precisely at the moment of publication that I am most aware of
my indebtedness to others. There is Prof. William R. Farmer, who
first introduced me to this question, and Prof. E. P. Sanders, who
suggested that I might find at McMaster University an environment
suitable for an open consideration of the genre question. Both men
have read the present text and have made many helpful suggestions
for its preparation. Also, Profs. D. M. Shepherd, Ben Meyer, and
David Dungan have read various stages of the work and offered valuable suggestions along the way. Finally, I am very much in debt to
Ms. Sue Bell Trickett who not only prepared the typed manuscript
but also served as a consultant in literary style. To each of these
persons, and to the others who must remain unnamed, I want to
express my deepest appreciation. In spite of the many contributions
heretofore stated and implied, however, it remains true that I alone
am responsible for the contents of the present work.

Philip L. Shuler
McMurry College

1

The Problem Under Consideration

The theory of books is noble. The scholar of the first age received into him the world around; brooded thereon; gave it the new arrangement of his own mind, and uttered it again. It came into him life; it went out from him truth. It came to him short-lived actions; it sent out from him immortal thoughts. . . . It was dead fact; now, it is quick thought. It can stand, and it can go. It now endures, it now flies, it now inspires. Precisely in proportion to the depth of mind from which it issued, so high does it soar, so long does it sing.[1]

In view of the wealth of research on the gospel narratives, it is strange that so fundamental an issue as the literary nature and character of the gospels should remain controversial. The purpose of the present book is to discuss this problem and the question of the genre or *Gattung*[2] of the gospels, particularly, Matthew's gospel. The first task, then, is to demonstrate that the genre question awaits a satisfactory solution.

A demonstration of the state of the question could be dealt with in either of two ways: a thorough review of the history of research on gospel genre or an examination of several key works which illustrate the critical issues of the problem. The historical approach would have the advantage of surveying previous discussions of the question, but the complexity of the problem would tend to make such a survey too time-consuming. Furthermore, however helpful, a detailed historical analysis would not, in our view, contribute significantly to the current task of formulating a new hypothesis concerning the generic nature of the gospels. For these reasons, therefore, the following overview of the primary issues related to gospel genre will focus on a discussion of four works by five scholars—C. W. Votaw, K. L. Schmidt, Moses Hadas and Morton Smith, and Charles Talbert—and the responses these works have generated.

THE GOSPELS AND POPULAR
BIOGRAPHY

In 1915, C. W. Votaw of the University of Chicago wrote an article, "The Gospels and Contemporary Biographies,"[3] which, since it predates the refinement of New Testament form criticism, illustrates one approach to the problem prior to form critical considerations. Votaw sought to relate the gospels as literary entities to classical and Hellenistic parallels. Since making comparisons of this kind is not common practice, it is important to take into account Votaw's view of the gospel narratives and the methodological presuppositions behind the comparisons he made.

Votaw's basic understanding of the nature of the gospel literature, is, in many ways, consistent with contemporary views. For example, he wrote the following:

> In character it [the gospel] was a religious tract, intended to promote the Christian movement. In style it represented the popular spoken language of the common people, for the author was not a trained philosopher or a professional littérateur.[4]

The gospels "were not intended to be a contribution to historical or philosophical literature," nor are they to be viewed as "historical writings produced by a historical impulse and method." Rather, they are to be viewed "as propagandist writings" of the early Christian movement. They are not called "Lives of Jesus," but "Gospels," that is, evangelistic literature promoting "Jesus as Christ, Lord, Savior, and Teacher to the Mediterranean world."[5] Few would argue with Votaw's assessment that "the Gospels are not chronicling but dramatic productions. They present pen pictures of Jesus as a divine Person on earth, revealing God, saving men, teaching righteousness, calling to repentance, healing sickness, heralding the new age . . . ." Their purpose is to enable men to "see Jesus . . . in the transfigured raiment of the son of God redeeming the world."[6]

Votaw did not feel that the above views of the nature of the gospel narratives precluded their comparison with other literature from that general period. Requisite for such comparisons, for him, however, was the recognition that there is a distinction between popular biography and historical biography and that the gospel narratives belong to the former category. Votaw proceeded carefully in establishing the legitimacy of his comparisons. He asked rhetorically: "Then are the Gospels *biographies* of Jesus?" His answer was, "No or yes, according to the connotation given the term 'biography.'" Then, in the following qualification of his "no or yes" answer, he presented his understanding of popular and historical biography:

> In the historical sense, a biography is a writing which aims to present all the important dates and facts about a person, with perspective and exactness, including his relation to other persons and to his times. This involves research, criticism, and interpretation, according to the current principles of history-writing. It is obvious that the Gospels are not biographies in this sense of the term.
>
> In the popular sense, a biography is any writing which aims to make one acquainted with a historical person by giving some account of his deeds and words, sketchily chosen and arranged, even when the motive of the writer is practical and hortatory rather than historical. The amount, character, order, and accuracy of the historical information contained in these pragmatic writings vary greatly, according to the purposes, interests, abilities, and resources of the several authors. The Gospels may be classified with productions of this kind; in the popular sense, they are biographies, and we commonly so think of them.[7]

Accordingly, the remainder of Votaw's article is devoted to a discussion of the similarities of the "portraits" contained in the gospels with those contained in Arrian's *Discourses of Epictetus,* Philostratus's *Life of Apollonius of Tyana,* and the works of both Xenophon and Plato which preserve traditions about Socrates. Votaw obviously believed that these works also belong to the "popular biography" category.

Methodologically, it is important to observe that the comparisons Votaw made were not derived from textual or form critical analysis of the sources behind the gospels. Rather, he was concerned with the image or portrait that evolved from the whole of the works chosen for examination. Comparisons were limited to the general purposes of the tracts, including the apologetic or didactic intentions of the authors, a consideration of the impact of the "hero" upon the society in which he lived and especially upon those disciples who were drawn to his side, an all-too-brief account of the hero's teachings, and references to biographical material insofar as biographical details were discernible (accomplishments, death, glorification, and so on). Votaw made no attempt to establish direct literary relationships or to outline any common pattern of development of either the hero's image or the particular type of literature from which the image emerged. His only assertion was that each of these examples falls into the same broad category of popular biography, and on this basis were such comparisons thought to be valid.

It is one thing to argue for a rationale behind one's comparisons; it is quite another to build a case for generic relations. If Votaw intended the latter, it is indeed regrettable that he did not spend more time verifying the existence of his "popular" and "historical" classifications of biography. It is precisely on this point that he becomes vulnerable; for genre requires more for verification than a rationale for literary comparison. First of all, there is reason to restrict the use of the term *biography*, since biography as a literary discipline is a relatively recent development. To be sure, there are numerous works dating back to the ancients which bear the title *bios* or *vita*, but none of these works may be referred to as "biography" in a modern sense— a fact which Votaw himself observes. To defend such a position now would require a detailed elaboration on the meaning and use of the term biography as a genre designation. Second, the use of the terms *popular* and *historical* creates problems for the New Testament exegete. It is true that the former term is frequently applied to the gospels with reference to the type of literature and the character of the audience to whom this literature is addressed. But if Votaw intended to identify a particular genre in which to classify the gospels, the basis upon which he argues for the existence of a popular, as distinct from an historical, biographical genre must be more convincingly stated. Where is the historical evidence for such genres during the period in which the gospels were written?

Closer examination leads to the conclusion that Votaw was not primarily concerned with the isolation of identifiable literary genres. He has not appealed to the rhetoricians for support of a genre, nor does he elaborate upon the "historical–popular" dichotomy except to show that his comparisons are methodologically sound. At several points he does use the term *memorabilia* in connection with traditions concerning Jesus' ministry. He writes, for example, "They contain historical reminiscences, or memorabilia, of Jesus' ministry; but for the practical use these may serve in the evangelistic mission."[8] For

Votaw, the gospel narratives contain memorabilia; they are not in themselves examples of memorabilia. His brief survey of ancient biographical writings illustrates the point that the ancients, like the gospel writers, sought to "portray" rather than to "photograph" in their literary compositions.[9] Thus Votaw was more concerned with the literary product and its application than with the questions of form and origin related to genre classification. Accordingly, he writes:

> It was the purpose of these writings to make known the personality and the message of these three great moral–religious teachers. The authors wrote with a practical, not with a chronicling intent. They did not make historical investigation, or give a systematic accurate account of the life, . . . but gave memorabilia of the teaching, with more or less incident in conjunction. . . . The message of each man was the thing of primary interest and value, together with the personality of the man behind his message. The events of his life, his genetic relationship to his environment, and his influence upon his times were secondary matters that received little or no attention. Therefore these lives of Epictetus, Apollonius, and Socrates, like the Gospels, are not biographies of the historical but of the popular type. They eulogize and idealize their heroes, they select their best sayings and interpret them for practical use, they give the memorabilia in an atmosphere of appreciation, they commend the message to the faith and practice of all.[10]

Elsewhere he writes:

> Obviously Socrates and Jesus are presented as public heroes, as exemplary persons to be appreciated and imitated. The primary motive of putting them before the public in writings is to instruct and to inspire men in their type of living. The interpretation of them given by the authors will be such as the practical end requires. Acts, utterances, and characteristics that have inspirational and pedagogical value will be selected and presented in an effective way. The hero will be read into the later environment of which the writer is a part, and will be arrayed to function for this environment, however it may differ from the conditions in which his own life was set. . . . The chief concern of their biographers was to accomplish practical results in the moral–religious sphere.[11]

It would seem, therefore, that Votaw's primary concern was not the definition of literary genres but rather the fruitful results to be gained from comparisons of the nature and function of the portraits which emerge from these writings taken as literary wholes. Such comparison, however, would soon be denied him by the work of Karl Ludwig Schmidt, to which we now turn our attention.

THE GOSPELS AND *KLEINLITERATUR*

In 1923, K. L. Schmidt set the tone for subsequent discussions of the genre of the gospels when his article, "Die Stellung der Evangelien in der allgemeinen Literaturgeschicte," was published in the Hermann Gunkel *Festschrift*.[12] Schmidt, whose purpose was to survey and evaluate the literature related to the question of the *Gattung* of the gospels, did not comment on the results of Votaw's comparisons, but he did not respond to the basis upon which such comparisons were made, thereby breaking the ground for his own position. Schmidt felt that Votaw and others had erred in their classifications of literature and in the proposed relationship of the gospels to these categories. His own categories were much more broadly conceived: *Hochliteratur* as distinct from *Kleinliteratur*. It is important that one understand fully what Schmidt meant by this dichotomy and its effect upon the question of gospel genre before examining its current usefulness.

For Schmidt, *Hochliteratur* included all literature in which the personality and artistic intentions of the "author" are clearly discernible. Style, structure, authorial intent, and literary skill are present in these works, at least in their design if not in the final results. In cases where the "author" is working with earlier sources, his literary tasks include the systematic collection, evaluation, editing, and organization of these smaller units into a predetermined narrative form. This form is the product of the author's creative design. In what may be called formal biography, for example, such factors as the perception of personality, statements concerning outward appearance, characterization, and indications of the hero's inner motivations are clearly evident. In memoirs, to cite another example, what Schmidt calls "the literary I" is dominant. At every point, Schmidt asserted that the gospels contained none of the identifiable characteristics of *Hochliteratur*.

Kleinliteratur, on the other hand, is synonymous with "folk" literature—that vast, loosely defined body of material consisting of small and often incoherently joined literary units. One cannot speak of an "author," because these units are given their form through a long process of oral transmission governed by universal laws; and the compilers, if and when these units are compiled, display little personal interest in systematic editing. They certainly do not impress themselves upon the materials. According to Schmidt, this manner of collecting materials produces a *Volksbuch*. These texts display evidence of revisions, amplifications, and even distortions which are the natural hazards of popular oral transmission. Even in book form, *Kleinliteratur* still possesses the mobility of the oral tradition which produced it. There is no "*Gattung* motive" and the accounts may be based upon living, popular, and cultic traditions. According to Schmidt, the gospels are *Kleinliteratur*.

Using the distinction between *Hochliteratur* and *Kleinliteratur*, Schmidt proceeded to refute every literary parallel with which the gospels had previously been compared. For example, Schmidt argued that the gospels could not be compared with such literary types as contemporary biography, autobiography, memoir materials, Rabbinic anecdotes, or history. Schmidt's readers repeatedly encounter the statement that one cannot make comparisons between *Hochliteratur* and *Kleinliteratur*. One can only draw valid conclusions from comparisons made within these respective categories; that is, the gospels can only be compared with other examples of *Kleinliteratur*. In effect, this position precludes comparisons with almost all literature of the period of the gospels because no examples of *Kleinliteratur* are available. Those cited for consideration by Schmidt included such cult and folk legends as the eighteenth-century Hasidic legends of the Great Maggid, traditions behind Doctor Faust, *Apophthegmata Patrum*, Franciscan legends, and a vast body of popular tradition preserved in a fifty-volume collection presently in Paris.[13] Schmidt claimed that, even though they are relatively late, it is only in examples of this type that one can see how the traditions of the gospels were circulated, collected, and finally written down. The gospels were created by the natural process of folk transmission, that is, they are *sui generis*.

The difference between Votaw's position and Schmidt's is clear. The primary problem is that, for Votaw, "popular" is not synonymous with "folk" literature. Obviously, for him, Arrian, Xenophon, and Plato were capable of producing historical and popular literature, of which the latter was directed toward the general public for entertainment, moral instruction, or related purposes. Votaw compared the gospels with accounts of heroes whose exponents deemed them worthy of the public's attention and contributive, by their example, to the public good. Schmidt's categories, on the other hand, were culturally and sociologically rooted. His view is rigid: Plato simply would not produce literature which could be classified with what Schmidt calls *Kleinliteratur*. Likewise, the gospel editors, however noble their efforts, were incapable of producing, or being directly influenced by, *Hochliteratur*. The positions of Votaw and Schmidt are irreconcilable.

In order to understand Schmidt's thesis properly, one should realize that it was developed in the context of form criticism, then a relatively new discipline whose emergence and acceptance were certainly enhanced by Schmidt's own contributions.[14] As early as 1882, Franz Overbeck had described the gospel narratives as "preliterary" (*Urliteratur*), noting especially their brief literary development and history.[15] In 1919, Martin Dibelius observed that the real distinction to be made in a study of literature must necessarily be between high and low forms; that is, between literary and nonliterary works. In *From Tradition to Gospel,* Dibelius described the synoptic gospels in the following manner: "Without a doubt these are unliterary writings (*Kleinliteratur*). They should not and cannot be compared with 'literary' works (*Hochliteratur*)."[16] Dibelius's characterization of *Kleinliteratur* was similar to that of Schmidt.[17] Popular traditions are handed down by many persons who remain anonymous. These anonymous persons, however, are not mere vehicles for the traditions, they introduce changes or additions without any evidence of "literary" intent at any stage. The peculiarities of the "composer or narrator" are not evident in the narrative. More evident is the form in which the traditions are transmitted, a form which itself is created "by practical necessities, by usage, or by origin." When the narrative undergoes development, it is the consequence of natural rules of transmission, "for no creative mind has worked upon the material and impressed it with his own personality."

Rudolf Bultmann agreed on this point. In his *History of the Synoptic Gospels,* Bultmann wrote, "It seems to me that while we need analogies for understanding the individual components of the Synoptic Tradition we do not need them for the Gospel as a whole." After all, "What analogies can be suggested?" The answer for Bultmann is "none in the *Greek Tradition*." The reason for this negative answer is clearly stated. The gospels display no "historical–biographical interest," which is "why they have nothing to say about Jesus' human personality, his appearance and character, his origin, education and development. . . ." The personalities of the authors are not projected into the texts, and these texts do not reflect the "cultivated techniques of composition necessary for grand literature (*hohe Literatur*)." Finally, the "literature of *memoirs and lives of the philosophers*" may be excluded from comparisons with the gospels, because the former have no link with myth and cult whereas the latter contain no scientific–historical interests.[18]

Thus it is in the context of the development of form criticism—the essential founders and exponents of which were in basic agreement about the generic nature of the gospels—that we can understand why the *sui generis* solution was applied to the character of the gospel narratives.[19] In particular, until recently, Schmidt's article removed the question of genre from the form critical concerns of gospel research, except in connection with the smaller literary units within the whole.

The position of Schmidt and the other form critics, as stated above, continues to surface in the discussions of the *Gattung* of the gospels, and a closer, more critical examination of Schmidt's premise is, therefore, necessary. Considered together, the discussion and arguments which follow demand a reevaluation of the question of gospel genre.

Interestingly enough, Dibelius himself saw problems with Schmidt's conclusions, even though his observations cannot be said to have altered his own views significantly. Dibelius was concerned with the relationship of gospel formation to those rules which govern the formulation and transmission of traditions in the oral stage of development. The question raised was, essentially, to what extent do the gospels reflect a literary development such as that presupposed by the transmission of popular traditions? Dibelius's conclusion was that general comparisons involving the history of tradition cannot yield conclusive results because of the vast difference of cultures, the remoteness of periods, and the variety of content in the traditions. We could add the inability of scholars to agree on those specific and general literary laws which govern popular transmission (against Schmidt and the examples of *Kleinliteratur* he cited). Nevertheless, Dibelius went on to accept Schmidt's work in general, stating that "it may suffice to hint at this broad, indeed boundless region."[20]

More recently, W. D. Davies recognized the problem of comparing the gospels with other forms of tradition in which general rules of transmission are said to exercise literary influence. Davies has accepted the contributions of form criticism in general but feels that it has been "unduly influenced" by the history of tradition in the Old Testament and in other folk literature. He writes:

> But any comparison between such literatures and the New Testament must be dubious. The Old Testament covers at least ten centuries; folk literature usually stretches over long periods of time. The New Testament, on the other hand, probably was all composed within a century. . . . The Gospels contain materials remembered recently, at least as compared with other traditional literatures, so that the rules which governed the transmission of folk tradition do not always apply to the tradition found in the Gospels.[21]

Davies raises the question whether sufficient time had elapsed between the events and the written record to allow universal or general rules to become functional in the formation of the gospel narratives. Davies's observation raises serious doubts about the degree to which the gospel narratives were shaped by the rules of popular transmission of the type implicit in Schmidt's understanding of *Kleinliteratur*.

E. P. Sanders, a pupil of Davies, has pointed to another important and not unrelated critical issue for those who would relate the laws of popular transmission to the gospel traditions. In *The Tendencies of the Synoptic Tradition*, Sanders observes that the universal tendencies of tradition and their comparisons with synoptic traditions have not been firmly and objectively established. He points to the unjustified assumption often held by form critics that the so-called laws of popular transmission have been derived from a study of the "course of development of traditions which, though non-Christian, parallel the Christian materials in type and age. . . ." The comparisons that have been made were done in order to understand formal characteristics of the tradition rather than to understand the changes made in the tradition at the various stages of development and transmission. Sanders's point is that the latter task "has never been done,"[22] which means, further, that the basis on which the so-called laws of popular transmission have been founded has yet to be convincingly established. One should note, therefore, that the emergence of the gospel narratives within the context of the Christian community and the manner in which these traditions were nurtured, developed, and presented prior to these written narratives are by no means settled issues; and Schmidt's position now appears to be vastly oversimplified. William O. Walker is indeed correct in his identification of several unresolved questions related to Matthew's gospel: "The unresolved questions include those relating to authorship, date, place and circumstances of composition, source or sources, and the *exact nature and duration of the process* which led from the primitive traditions about Jesus to the appearance of the Gospel According to Matthew."[23] There are numerous questions surrounding the laws of transmission of the gospel traditions which, though thought by Schmidt and others to have been settled, are, in fact, yet to be resolved.

Even more problematic for the present writer is the mechanical manner in which the terms *Hochliteratur* and *Kleinliteratur*—categories initially employed in the study of medieval literature—have been used to invalidate all literary comparisons with the gospels. One senses that Schmidt is working with a thesis already presumed true, which is the grounds for disqualifying all theories that the gospels are literary units. The distinction between *Hochliteratur* and *Kleinliteratur* is not itself objectionable. No doubt the ancient world did produce "high" and "low" forms of literature, but it also, doubtless, produced a great deal which would lie somewhere in between (an assertion which must, in the final analysis, remain speculative because of the relatively small body of evidence preserved from the periods in question). This is precisely the objection—here is a hypothesis which does not admit the possibility of anything lying in between these two poles, one which presupposes the mutual exclusiveness of the two categories. F. C. Grant describes the situation of the gospels more accurately when he writes that even though the earliest Christians were not, for the most part, an educated group, "their very language when they did come to write, was . . . the language of the masses; not illiterate, but certainly nonliterary."[24]

Though the observation, "not illiterate, but certainly nonliterary," is perhaps true, it is doubtful that it legitimately precludes the type of comparisons Votaw made in favor of the exclusive categories utilized by Schmidt. For the present writer, it is precisely Schmidt's exclusiveness, and that of others after him, which is to be questioned. An illustration may clarify this objection. When Lucian wrote his essay *How to Write History*, he was disturbed about the methods of some contemporary historians.[25] Many writers were calling their works "histories," but the result, according to Lucian, left much to be desired.

Apparently, it was common practice to distort, amplify, and even omit for the sake of creating good impressions. Lucian felt this was not good historical procedure, and his essay was intended to correct the situation. No doubt now all would agree with Lucian's rejection of these works as responsible historical accounts. From what Lucian says about them, it would also be difficult for us to call them biographies. But, by the same token, one cannot deny these works the status of literature, regardless of how widely they miss the literary mark. Nor can their literary character be denied simply because they were obviously addressed to the populace. Here we encounter the difficulty of applying Schmidt's dichotomy. Were the terms *Hochliteratur* and *Kleinliteratur* familiar to Lucian, he would no doubt have applied the latter designation to the works in question.[26] Schmidt, on the other hand, would more than likely have placed them in the *Hochliteratur* category on the basis of the literary intent associated with the pretense of writing "history." What appears actually to be the case is that Lucian is dealing with a form of laudatory oratory which, in the case of those against whom he is writing, is designed to please and entertain at the expense of accuracy. The results may even have been "nonliterary" when measured against literary models, but these works were obviously not produced by illiterate practitioners.

This example illustrates that Schmidt's dichotomy inadequately represents the situation, which is more complex than the radical application of the two categories admits. Consequently, use of either *Hochliteratur* or *Kleinliteratur* in connection with the works which Lucian is attacking produces an assessment which is only partially correct. Were these categories commonplace for Lucian, he would perhaps have made one judgment and his antagonists another, whereas a modern reader might disagree with both. The *Hochliteratur* and *Kleinliteratur* dichotomy, therefore, is of little assistance to a discussion of the problem of gospel genre;[27] on the contrary, the distinction, when applied rigorously, works against a solution by radically limiting the options.[28]

In addition to what may be said directly of K. L. Schmidt's work, recent trends in New Testament scholarship which are relevant to Schmidt's thesis must also be taken into consideration. Although the emphasis of form criticism continues to be on the smaller literary pericopes, the practitioners of the discipline commonly referred to as

Redaktionsgeschichte[29] have attached considerable importance to the presence of the "redactor" or "editor" of the gospel narratives. It is now widely recognized that these unknown editors exercised considerable choice in both the selection and the structuring of the materials available to them. The emphases imposed upon each gospel by its editor are discernible in an analysis of their redactional (that is, editorial) techniques. Scholars now proceed in the belief that the purposes and theologies of the gospel writers may be discussed objectively, a fact which challenges Schmidt's view of the complete anonymity and impersonal structuring of the synoptic narratives. It is through an analysis of the literary choices these editors made—their additions, omissions, amplifications, and arrangement—that adherents of *Redaktionsgeschichte* arrive at the literary presence of those responsible for the present form of the gospels. Thompson, for example, describes his task in the following manner:

> I call myself a composition-critic rather than a redaction-critic. My basic methodological presupposition is that Matthew's editorial activity—whether it be called redaction or composition—was so thorough-going and proceeded out of such a unique vision that it transformed all that he touched.[30]

It is clear, therefore, that the acceptance of the results and methodology of this discipline necessitates considerable modification, if not a complete overhaul, of Schmidt's understanding of those forces present in the formation of the gospel narratives.

Wherever in gospel studies one begins to work, one must sooner or later come to grips with the *bios* factor (that is, the literary procedure by which traditions related to Jesus are presented in narratives about Jesus which are so structured as to be highly suggestive of biographical literature). One may, with Schmidt, reject the term *biography*. One may insist upon referring to the gospels as nonliterary. The *bios* factor nevertheless remains dominant in these narratives, whose major focus is Jesus of Nazareth. This concern may be traced to the editors of the gospel texts, for they could easily have rejected the *bios* aspect for a less personal format (such as collections of sayings, miracles, and epiphanies, which demonstrate little interest in a "beginning" and "conclusion").[31] The question is, what accounts for such a *bios* factor and its thematic development within the gospels?[32]

The most common explanation is that the *bios* factor was important because of its germinal presence in the *kerygma*. Along with Dibelius and Bultmann, Schmidt anticipated this explanation by emphasizing the cultic character of the gospels. Julius Schniewind was the first to conclude that the gospels assumed their present form because their essential ingredients (*Vorformen*) were already contained in the kerygma.[33] The gospels were said to have given "the kerygma a definite place and task," and this is to be seen in the "theological character of the Gospels." The *new quest* for the historical Jesus continued to follow Schniewind in this emphasis upon the kerygma in gospel formation. James Robinson states emphatically that "in the narrative, just as in the *kerygma*, we are confronted with paradox: exaltation in humiliation, life in death, the kingdom of God in the present evil aeon, the eschatological in history." In fact, this kerygma, for Robinson, "is constitutive of the Gospel as a literary form."[34] In his attempt to convey the proper relationship between "Gospel," "kerygma," and "history," Robinson is very close to Schniewind: "The Gospels . . . do not present the historical Jesus in distinction from *kerygma*, but rather present a kerygmatized history of Jesus."[35] He continues by saying that the important point is not "whether the *kerygma* preserves detailed historical memories about Jesus" but that it is "decidedly an evaluation of the historical person."

Helmut Koester[36] also adopted the views of Schniewind, and he explicitly states that the form of the gospels cannot be explained in any other way than the one proposed by Schniewind: "It is, in fact, a creation of the kerygma of the early Christian community." It is precisely this kerygma that "has made the written Gospel a genuinely Christian type of literature."[37] Koester therefore maintains, with Schmidt, that the gospels are distinctively Christian, that is, their literary form has no forerunners nor contemporary parallels. He describes them as pseudobiographical rather than biographical, because the outlines of Jesus' life provide the framework for the sayings and narratives and are "actually an extension of the kerygma of Jesus' passion and resurrection."[38] Having thus affirmed his thesis of the theological motivation inherent in the formation of these narratives, Koester discusses this "theological motif" in terms of the earliest literary genres which preserved the Christian community's traditions about Jesus. These include collections of sayings, aretalogies, revelation discourses, and even some of the creedal affirmations of the second century. His thesis is that, although the gospel form combines several genres, the resulting narrative does not reflect any literary type outside the *Christian* (cult) milieu.

Schmidt and Schniewind and Robinson and Koester are correct in their respective emphases, but they do not explain convincingly how the kerygma could have been expanded so as to accommodate so strong a *bios* form. It is recognized that, at the time of the composition of the gospels, collections of sayings and perhaps miracles as well as verbal proclamations of the death and resurrection of Jesus were already in circulation. In this light, the arguments of Schmidt and Schniewind and of Robinson and Koester are insufficient to explain the dramatized accounts that appear as "gospels," however incomplete the drama may appear in each instance.[39]

It becomes increasingly clear that, in addition to the internal weaknesses of Schmidt's argument, two other factors have emerged as a result of current trends in gospel studies: (1) an editor–redactor–author who did exercise considerable control over the formulation and organization of his materials and (2) a pervasive *bios* factor which controls the narrative form.

ARETALOGY AND MYTH

One recent attempt to relate the gospel narratives to a biographical literary form known as the aretalogy was a joint project undertaken by Moses Hadas and Morton Smith. *Heroes and Gods: Spiritual Biographies in Antiquity* fully took into account not only the presence of an editor–redactor but also the controlling influence of the *bios* factor in the gospel literature. An aretalogy is initially defined as a "formal account of the remarkable career of an impressive teacher that was used as a basis for moral instruction."[40] Often an aretalogy recounts the preternatural gifts of the teacher and the teachings which made him famous. Fame is often accompanied by conflict with established authorities "whom he [the hero] confronted with courage and at whose hands he suffered martyrdom."[41] Frequently, the subject of an aretalogy works wonders and magnetically gathers about him a following of devoted disciples "committed to propagating the teaching of the master."[42] The central figure of the aretalogy could not be described as a mere "hero." "He is consistently and intentionally benevolent

and free from the stark passions so often inseparable from the ordinary hero's virtues," and his qualities are of a "spiritual, not material
order."[43] These qualities include a continuous healing of souls and
teaching "by example as well as by precept."[44] So elevated an individual often acquires cultic significance, and, when this happens, he
embodies the highest ideals for which one could strive within the
cultic community. According to Hadas, one can see the impact of the
poets upon aretalogy and trace its development through Dionysius,
Heracles, Theseus, Orpheus, Pythagoras, Empedocles, and the Socrates of Plato. After Plato, aretalogy developed in two ways, with the
stress on the more scientific elements of *bios* or aretalogical literature, influenced by Aristotle and the Peripatetics, and with the more
spiritual emphases of the Hellenistic schools, such as the Epicureans
and the Stoics. The stories of the reforming kings of the third century
B.C. reflect much of what is contained in aretalogy, and Dio Chrysos-
tom's "The Hunters of Euboea" and the plots of the romances, among
others, became important links in the development of aretalogy.

Many of the figures mentioned by Hadas and Smith reportedly
died as martyrs, which is common in cultic traditions. According to
Hadas, "A martyrdom is in effect an aretalogy, and if it gives largest
place to the holy man's heroism under persecution and his glorious
death, that is because the death is after all the crown of the career."[45]
In the second portion of the book, Smith presented for consideration
four works which were said to reflect clearly the aretalogical tradition:
Porphyry's *The Life of Pythagoras* and excerpts from Philo's *On the
Life of Moses*," "The Gospel According to Luke," and Philostratus's
The Life of Apollonius of Tyana.

Hadas and Smith's work is important because it presents a type of
bios literature whose examples could clarify the problem of the literary form of the gospels, although not everyone is willing to accept this
thesis as it is further supported by Smith.[46] One problem is the absence of clear aretalogical examples for investigation. To his credit,
Hadas is the first to admit this difficulty:

> After so elaborate a preamble it is something of an anticlimax to have to
> acknowledge that we have no complete text surviving from the past
> specifically labelled aretalogy, and indeed that the word is hardly recog-
> nized in our standard dictionaries; but there can be no reasonable doubt
> that the thing and its name once had currency. We know that the careers
> of holy men were given literary form in order to serve as a basis for

moral instruction because vestiges and adaptations of such works are recognizable in certain biographical and other writings that have in fact survived.[47]

Hadas can show only indirectly that aretalogy constitutes a literary genre, citing only examples of what aretalogy might be if such were available. All four translated examples are comparatively late for verifying the existence of a literary genre prior to the gospels. Porphyry wrote in the middle of the third century A.D., Philo in the first half of the first century A.D., and Luke in the second half of the same century. Philostratus's work is no earlier. In addition, three of these examples contain the designation, *bios,* while the fourth is an account in which "proclaiming the gospel" is as close as one gets to the designation "gospel." In all of these cases, antecedents would seem to be found not in early aretalogies as described by Hadas and Smith, but in early biographical or similarly related forms of literature. This raises the question as to what distinguishes aretalogies from other biographical types. Is it the vocation of the subject, the scope of the undertaking in terms of *topoi* to be presented, or some other criterion? Hadas himself infers the existence of the term *aretalogy* from his study of the use of the Latin term *aretalogus* and the Greek equivalent, *aretas legein.*[48] H. C. Kee has challenged the existence of the aretalogical form by noting that neither the examples translated by Smith nor the gospels contain all the essential ingredients of aretalogy.[49] It is, therefore, one thing to say that the result of the efforts of the gospel writers may be described as aretalogical; it is quite another to affirm that the form of the gospels has been influenced by an aretalogy whose generic existence is textually uncertain and which cannot, therefore, be subject to literary examination.

This questioning of the existence of an aretalogical genre means only that its existence as a biographical form, as presented by Hadas and Smith, is disputable. Hadas and Smith's reconstruction nevertheless remains one option in an attempt to relate the gospels directly to ancient biographical literature.[50] Others who have examined aretalogical traditions in relation to the gospels discuss aretalogical traditions more in terms of motif than *bios* form. Generally speaking, aretalogies of this type are usually associated with the careers and accomplishments of individuals who have been attributed a divine status, hence the "divine man" (*theios aner*) concept.

Posited relationships between the gospels and aretalogies so understood have proved more acceptable than those involving aretalogies as more broadly defined by Hadas and Smith. Koester's article, for example, includes a section which is specifically titled "Jesus as the Divine Man (Aretalogies)."[51] H.-D. Betz's article under a similar title discusses the understanding of *theios aner* implicit in the gospels.[52] A brief quotation from Koester's work illustrates this:

> In such primitive gospel sources Jesus appears as a man endowed with divine power who performs miracles to prove his divine quality and character. . . . Aretalogies were normally written for purposes of religious propaganda, . . . these stories of extraordinary events and performances represent in themselves the essential creed and belief of a religious movement. Gospels in the form of aretalogies, such as the miracle sources of Mark and John, proclaim that a particular divine power is present and available in these powerful acts of Jesus.[53]

Essential to this understanding of aretalogy is not literary pattern or form per se, but rather the relation of the individual traditions to the *theios aner* whose authority is chiefly derived from miracles. The aretalogy of which Koester speaks may be in the form of a collection of miraculous stories and events or even in the form of a letter of recommendation based upon the miracle.[54] There have also been commendable attempts to reconstruct a composite view of the *theios aner*;[55] but, as D. L. Tiede has shown, the value of these reconstructions is limited in that the result is constructed from many different sources. Consequently, the notion that there is a single, prevailing understanding of the concept of "divine man" is somewhat misleading.[56] There is no account of a divine man which corresponds to those reconstructed from all the evidence related to the *theios aner* concept. For the most part, therefore, aretalogies of divine men (with the exception of Hadas and Smith's interpretation) do not reflect a primary concern for a "life" of the divine man. They are collections or traditions about the *theios aner* which relate his supranatural powers.

Robinson was one of the earliest to associate the aretalogy with the development of the gospel form.[57] He presupposed the priority of Mark and explained the gospel form in terms of a process of literary evolution. His thesis refers to the "Signs Source" in John's gospel which he uses to detect a "pre-Marcan stage in the morphology of the *Gattung*."[58] The "Signs (miracle) Source" (or sources), therefore, is thought to be evident in both Mark and John.[59] The significance of this source is stated thus by Robinson: "The Signs Source shows with all clarity Jesus being assimilated to the *theios aner* ideal of the Hellenistic miracle worker or faith healer."[60] Robinson explains the emergence of the gospel form in the following way:

> Kähler's definition of Mark as a passion narrative with a long introduction together with form criticism's recognition that the only sizable part of the tradition that had been held together as a unit prior to Mark was the passion narrative, had tended to cast Mark's role in the creation of the gospel *Gattung* into that of simply prefixing to the passion narrative oral materials without really explaining the origin of this "introduction" in terms of *Gattung*. But the parallel of the Signs Source might suggest that (somewhat in analogy to Matthew and Luke imbedding Q in Mark and thus blocking the gnosticizing proclivities of saying sources leading to the Gospels of Thomas and Philip) Mark (and John) blunted the proclivities of collections of miracle stories (leading to apocryphal acts and infancy narratives like that of Thomas . . .) by connecting this material with the passion narrative by means of the secrecy motif—a *tour de force* that has left scars especially in chapter 8.[61]

Thus, according to Robinson, by softening the aretalogical character of a body of "Jesus tradition" (closely resembling, if not identical with, that of the Signs Source in John's Gospel) through the use of both the secrecy motif and the addition of the passion narrative, the Gospel of Mark came into existence, that is, it "emerged." It is now clear that, in contrast with Hadas and Smith, Koester, Betz, and Robinson do not see aretalogy as the key to the question of gospel genre.

We are now prepared to see the complexity of the problem of isolating an "aretalogy." Tiede puts his finger on the real difficulty: "There appears to be no unified picture of what constituted an aretalogy in the ancient world."[62] As Tiede's study continues, it becomes apparent that aretalogical structures, *topoi*, and techniques differ so greatly that no uniform pattern emerges.[63] In his attempt to provide an intelligible understanding of the aretalogical traditions of the ancient world, Tiede offers two general types: the aretalogy whose authority was based primarily upon the miraculous and that whose authority was derived from philosophy. In fact, these types might be better understood as poles between which aretalogies tended to vacillate. Given its complexity, neither the concept of aretalogy presented by Hadas and Smith nor that of Koester and Robinson is necessarily incorrect. The problem with the former, as stated, is the absence of clear examples with which the gospels may be compared. The essential problem with the latter is that it amounts to only a partial explanation and, as noted, fails to account sufficiently for the *bios* factor in the gospels.

In conclusion, therefore, it is clear that there is still much work to be done before the impact of the aretalogical tradition (or specific type) on the formation of the gospels can be measured.

A more recent attempt to explain the *bios* factor within the formal structure of the gospels is Charles Talbert's *What Is a Gospel?: The Genre of the Canonical Gospels*.[64] After a brief introduction to the problem, Talbert focuses upon Bultmann's threefold argument against the view that the gospels belong to the biographical genre of the ancient world: (1) the gospels are mythical but the Greco–Roman biographies are not; (2) the gospels are cultic and the Greco–Roman biographies are not; and (3) whereas the gospels emerge from a community with a world-negating outlook, the literary biographies are produced by and for a world-affirming people. Talbert accepts the first half of arguments 1 and 2 and then convincingly argues that Greco–Roman biographies *are* dominated by myth and that they *do* share cultic functions. With respect to Bultmann's third argument, Talbert admits the eschatological mood of the gospels but argues that the dominant attitude of the Greco–Roman biographies is also shared by the gospels, that is, the intent to clarify or further enrich earlier literary presentations of the hero of their narratives. Talbert concludes that the gospels are biographies, "albeit ancient ones."

Talbert's explanation for the *bios* factor is based on his convincingly argued premise that myth permeates both the gospels and much Greco–Roman biographical literature. His thesis is that myth provides the formal *bios* structure for the gospels: the myth of the immortal in the synoptic gospels and the Katabasis–Anabasis myth in John's gospel. He also suggests that social function should become the new basis for genre determination. On this basis, he posits five biographical types in the ancient world: (A) works which "provide the readers a pattern to copy"; (B) lives which "aim to dispel a false image of the teacher," thereby providing a true model to follow; (C) lives which attempt to "discredit a given teacher by exposé"; (D) lives of philosophers which indicate "where the 'living voice' was to be found" in the line of succession after the period of the founder; and (E) lives of philosophers which intend to validate or provide the hermeneutical key for the teacher's doctrine, or both.

Talbert's work is to be commended, and his polemic against Bultmann is persuasive. The main problem is what Talbert has not done. Whereas he has shown that the gospels are mythical (along with numerous ancient biographical narratives) and cultic (also as ancient biographies) and that they correct and enrich previous tradition, he has not specifically demonstrated that those conventions shared by the gospels are common to ancient biographical narratives (that is, those "shared conventions" which comprise a literary genre). The logic of his work is that if it can be shown that myth provides the structure of the gospels, and if that same myth can be shown to have been prominent in ancient biographical works, then the gospels are of the same genre if Bultmann's other ingredients, cult and mood, are present. What is lacking is a clear understanding of that system of shared conventions that constitutes "ancient biography."[65] In order to conclude, as Talbert has done, that the gospels are biographies, one must further demonstrate that they are biographical in the same way that other ancient works, with or without myth, are considered biographical. Bultmann's other criticisms[66] and the work of K. L. Schmidt[67] require a closer examination of the gospels in relation to those shared conventions (including *topoi* and techniques) which, when combined, warrant the generic title "biography."

Furthermore, there are problems with Talbert's proposal that social function be the basis for genre determination. In support of Talbert's position, it should be emphasized that social function was important for those who wrote about famous people. For example, Talbert's type A (which is intended to provide a pattern) corresponds to the rhetorical rules of epideictic oratory which prescribe how a person is to be praised. Category C (discrediting a teacher) is similar to the rules for censure. In these two instances there are formal as well as functional grounds for Talbert's categories. How much further one can go is highly questionable. How, for example, can one separate Lucian's claim to develop "a pattern from our modern world" of "the best of all the philosophers" from his apologetic motive in *Demonax*? Talbert says it belongs to type A; there is also a strong case for type B. The problem is further illustrated in classification of the gospels. On the one hand, all the gospels belong to type B; on the other hand,

Mark and John belong to type B, Matthew belongs to type E; and Luke–Acts belongs to type D. It can be further argued that Luke provides the hermeneutical key to Acts and, therefore, belongs more to type E than to type D.[68] It is apparent that only a fine line separates these reconstructed types. One also suspects that these literary types, especially type B, are derived more from theories about the gospels than from identifiable literary qualities.[69]

Talbert's focus on myth and his discussion of Bultmann's threefold argument are important contributions to the discussion of the genre of the gospels. The question of the biographical nature of the gospels, however, remains unanswered.

SUMMARY

The following conclusions have been drawn from the brief survey of the problem of genre reflected in the writings of Votaw, Schmidt, Hadas and Smith, and Talbert.

Whereas Votaw's distinction between historical and popular biography may be questioned, this does not necessarily invalidate his methodological approach or the substance of the comparisons he made. His basic understanding of the gospel literature is sound, but a more legitimate basis for the comparisons of the gospels with classical texts needs to be developed.

Schmidt argues correctly that the gospels are unique in literature, but recognition of this uniqueness does not mean that they are *sui generis*. The *Hochliteratur* and *Kleinliteratur* dichotomy may, in retrospect, reflect the literary poles between which all ancient literature would fall, but the radical application of these terms, understood sociologically and separating "folk" from literary concerns, does not clarify the problem of gospel genre. It is now recognized that the editors exercised considerable literary skill in their deliberate choice and arrangement of traditions included in the present texts of the gospels. It is true that these narratives are kerygmatic, but it has not been demonstrated satisfactorily from a literary standpoint exactly how the kerygma could have been expanded to produce the present form of the gospel narratives. Such an explanation must account for the literary procedures of the production of the gospels, taking fully into account the dominant presence of the cult and the kerygma, and, at the same time, explaining the *bios* form these narratives assumed.

Hadas's and Smith's suggestion of the relationship of aretalogies with the gospels and Talbert's analysis of myth are more adequate explanations of the *bios* factor in the gospels. The Hadas and Smith position is hampered by the absence of a sufficient number of examples to establish conclusively the existence of such a genre, and the recently recognized complexities resulting from the variety of aretalogical traditions make difficult the acceptance of this solution. The Hadas and Smith proposal is appealing because it accounts for the biographical character of the gospel literature and offers a reasonable explanation for the movement of the church's kerygmatic proclamation in the direction of a *bios* presentation. The majority of those who have worked with aretalogical traditions, however, have stopped far short of positing a literary genre of the type proposed by Hadas and Smith. Talbert's work, on the other hand, explains how the kerygma and myth are combined in the gospels but fails to account sufficiently for the biographical nature of the gospels in terms of shared literary convention. Talbert has, however, moved the discussion forward by his demonstration of myth and cult in ancient biographical literature.

What has been established thus far is that the genre of the gospels remains a problem. In an attempt to address this problem, a different and, in some respects, more basic approach will be considered.

2

A Genre for the Gospels

Classification is a mode of naming, and I have enough empathy with the elementary principle of meaning to desire that names assigned in classifying do their jobs—the exerting of a certain amount of linguistic control over entities. For our purposes we speak of names of genres and mean thereby to identify the specific types of literature. Concern for the *genre littéraire* of a literary piece is part of one's historical–critical apperception of that text, and regulates attention given to it by recognizing the variability of possible hermeneutical starting points.[1]

The present chapter will address directly the problem of identifying a suitable genre for the gospels, one contemporary with the evangelists. This part of the discussion will begin with a statement of what is meant by the term *genre* and of how we understand the concept of a literary genre to be related to the individual works that are classified within a specific genre. Following this, we shall argue that there was a genre of laudatory biography common in antiquity, evidence of whose existence is the fact that it is consistently contrasted with the discipline of history writing. Further, it is our view that the chief characteristics of this genre may be discerned by references to the works of the rhetoricians who discuss epideictic oratory and, in particular, the genre *encomium*. It is our thesis that the gospels are related to the "encomium" biography understood as a literary genre. We begin with a brief discussion of the nature of a literary genre.

ASPECTS OF A LITERARY GENRE

Pattern

Arnaldo Momigliano has defined biography as "an account of the life of a man from birth to death."[2] On the surface, this definition of the literary genre appears oversimplified almost to the point of being ludicrous. It becomes clear, however, that Momigliano defines it in

24

this way in order to remove from consideration, and hence from his discussion, the definition of *how* one writes a biography. In effect, he elevates the level of the discussion and broadens the subject matter to embrace a proper consideration of genre, thereby rejecting (and rightly so) the notion that a literary genre can be determined by discussing how a particular narrative should be written.

For the present work, the term *genre* is intended to convey the concept of pattern implicit in the contents of a text and its affinities with other texts whose contents mediate similar patterns. Terms other than *pattern* could be employed. For example, Rene Wellek and Austin Warren define genre in the following way:

> Theory of genres is a principle of order: it classifies literature and literary history not by time or place (period or national language) but by specifically literary types of organization or structure.[3]

Likewise, William Doty prefers the term *structure*:

> The genre of any given text is made available to us only in the structure and configuration of the whole; the genre of a text is that which is characteristic of the whole yet in common with other texts sharing those characteristics.[4]

Although either term, pattern or structure, could be acceptable, the former appears to the present writer to be more appropriate.

Dynamic

Genre criticism must begin with the realization that genre is a dynamic, not a static, concept. This means that one may find variety within a single genre. Indeed, variety can be the basis of the formation of subgenres or even new genres. Wellek and Warren testify to this dynamic aspect of genre: "Do genres remain fixed? Presumably not. With the addition of new works, our categories shift."[5] Creativity within literary genres often consists of the appropriation and reshaping of existing genres or their characteristics, that is, internal change accommodating the desires of the particular author. This dynamism appears to be characteristic of classical as well as more modern genres (with which Wellek and Warren are primarily concerned) even if to a lesser degree. After noting that there are distinctive differences between "classical" and modern genre theory, Wellek and Warren write that "classical theory is regulative and prescriptive, though its

'rules' are not the silly authoritarianism still often attributed to them."[6]
The reservation implicit in the phrase "not the silly authoritarianism"
should be noted, for the ancients were also refining and, in some
instances, producing new genres through their literary efforts, even
while adhering to the prescriptions before them.[7] For example, the
differentiation of oratorical types is often made in terms of occasion,
place, and audience rather than prescriptive form and content.[8]

The variations between genres and the variety of genres found in
different cultures also demand that genres be understood as dynamic.
Genres often interact, even at relatively early stages of their development. "Every 'culture' has its genres: the Chinese, the Arabian,
the Irish; there are primitive oral 'kinds.' Medieval literature abound-
ed in kinds. We have no need to defend the 'ultimate' character of
the Greco–Roman kinds."[9] This multiplicity prevents one from speaking legitimately of the "perfection" of a specific genre,[10] for a genre will
be employed differently even by different persons within a given
culture, and the disparity between cultures and periods will be much
greater. Furthermore, it is often difficult to establish the exact relationship between one genre and a comparable one of a different
culture and period. The genre critic must, therefore, discern the
criteria relevant to a specific historical context in order to achieve
convincing results. For example, we have already noted the use of
the term *biography* as a broadly conceived literary type capable of
transcending temporal and cultural limitations. But it is unwarranted
to assume that the meaning and conventions conveyed by the term
were universal. In the Greco–Roman culture, for example, the term
was virtually nonexistent until quite late. The question, then, for the
genre critic is what, in this period, did their *bioi/vitae* denote when
written down, and what were the objectives of such treatises. In
other words, such works must be taken in the context of the milieu in
which they were conceived and to which they were addressed.

One of the reasons Willi Marxsen gives for excluding the gospels
from the category of biography is the "absence of everything required
for a biography (sequence of events, development, descriptions of
Jesus' appearance, and so on.)"[11] As Rudolf Bultmann put it, "they have
nothing to say about Jesus' human personality, his appearance and
character, his origin, education and development . . . ."[12] Bultmann

and Marxsen are implying that "biographies" in the first century had such characteristics. But is this true? Do these observations accurately describe the biographical genre or genres of that period? The contrast intended by Marxsen and Bultmann would be relevant if its purpose were to differentiate gospel literature from contemporary biographical works. But this is obviously not the point; consequently, these observations create the false impression that what is said to be lacking in the gospels is present in and, indeed, requisite for *ancient bios* narratives. Momigliano, to the contrary, has stated:

> As I have already hinted, we have no reason to believe that "literarishes Porträt," "Individualität," "Persönlichkeit," and so forth, are terms which can be transferred to the Greek and Roman world without a great deal of explaining—even explaining away.[13]

Even more pointedly, G. N. Stanton has recently examined the statements of Bultmann and Marxsen (and others) and has demonstrated convincingly that concerns for chronology, direct characterization, development, and placing the "hero" against the wider background of his time are not requisite for ancient biographical literature as was heretofore believed.[14] These examples indicate the pitfalls of applying universal concepts without properly acknowledging how each literary product served its particular milieu. The very notion of literary genre, therefore, entails continuity and discontinuity, freedom and authoritarianism, and newness in literary flux within a given environment. It is to be emphasized that continuity does not mean conformity to a set of universal rules. As a final example, the works of Diogenes Laertius, who is recognized as a collector of philosophical traditions but whose accounts do not emphasize sequence, development, appearance, and other such details, could not be included among ancient biographical works if Bultmann's criteria for biographical intent were accepted. But the genre critic's task is surely to discern in what way Diogenes Laertius's works belong to *bios* categories rather than to judge him by criteria irrelevant to his period or culture.

Finally, genre criticism has also come to realize that, because of the dynamic character implicit in the theory of genre, new genres are not created in a literary vacuum, that is, they cannot be *sui generis*. New genres emerge through the use of existing patterns and methods under different circumstances or for different purposes. One of the most cogent statements of the process by which a new genre is formed appears in E. D. Hirsch's treatment of "The Concept of Genre":

> This is one of the many penetrating observations that E. H. Gombrich makes in his book, *Art and Illusion*. He quotes approvingly Quintilian's remark, "Which craftsman has not made a vessel of a shape he has never seen?" and comments: "It is an important reminder, but it does not account for the fact that even the shape of the new vessel will somehow belong to the same family of forms as those the craftsman has seen." This tendency of the mind to use old types as the foundation for new ones is, of course, even more pronounced when communication or representation is involved. Not every convention could be changed all at once, even if the craftsman were capable of such divine creativity, because then his creation would be totally incommunicable, radically ambiguous. The point is stated pithily by Gombrich: "Variants can be controlled and checked only against a set of invariants."[15]

In a similar way, Wellek and Warren have observed: "The totally familiar and repetitive pattern is boring; the totally novel form will be unintelligible—is indeed unthinkable." Accordingly, "the genre represents, so to speak, a sum of aesthetic devices at hand, available to the writer and already intelligible to the reader."[16] Wellek and Warren then describe the "good writer" as one who "partly conforms to the genre as it exists" and "partly stretches" it. Furthermore, "great writers are not the inventors of genres," rather they "enter into other men's labours." Thus newness is accounted for by the process of the internal movement's becoming externalized because it can no longer be contained within a given genre. One of the tasks of genre criticism is to understand the development of the pattern being communicated by the writer. Doty is surely correct in stating, "Part of the tracing of generic viability involves not only the ways in which authors respond to available patterns, but how such adaptation of patterns is *received*."[17]

Genre and Form

In addition to the dynamic character of literary genre, it must be emphasized that the investigation of genre transcends the analysis of form. This is seen in Momigliano's definition of biography (see above) in which he expresses concern over the dominance of how-to-write questions in the discussions of genre. Doty proceeds similarly, stating, "Unless formal/structural criteria are explicitly stated, . . . genre tends to be equated with form."[18] In the absence of these criteria, such an equation can at best result in partial truth, for genre encompasses much more than the mere notion of form. This has been expressed by Wellek and Warren in terms of "inner" and "outer" forms.

> Genre should be conceived, we think, as a grouping of literary works based, theoretically, upon both outer form (specific metre or structure) and also upon inner form (attitude, tone, purpose—more crudely, subject and audience). The ostensible basis may be one or the other; . . . but the critical problem will then be to find the *other* dimension, to complete the diagram.[19]

In New Testament scholarship, the choice of terminology is critical in the study of generic relationships. With the development of form criticism in the twenties and its application to gospel studies, form was largely limited to the smaller literary units, for "the whole" was considered relatively formless. Form, then, denoted those recurrent formal elements which constituted a pericope, thus acquiring a tech-nical connotation comparable to what Wellek and Warren call outer form. It is partly for this reason that *Redaktionsgeschichte* has been received as a refreshingly new approach to the study of the gospels. Likewise, it is from this understanding that genre criticism has received renewed emphasis and from this same understanding that it will have to be disengaged in order to blossom afresh.[20] It is primarily because of the technical status the word *form* has assumed in its application to gospel studies that we prefer the term *pattern,* in discussions of the theory of genres, over the more natural terms *form* and *structure.*[21]

Genre, therefore, as the determining principle of the whole, may encompass a variety of forms, motifs, and themes—that is, smaller (in the sense of "smaller than the whole") literary units which may be employed in differing sequences according to the author's skill and purpose. Rigid compliance with form is not necessarily characteristic of any particular genre; rather, an author conveys his or her intended meanings by how he or she both complies with and digresses from a pattern said to be common in a particular genre. The genre critic, therefore, will take note of recurring forms, but he or she will hesi-tate to define them as arbitrarily requisite for a specific genre. Pattern may be demonstrable in different literary works regardless of whether or not B always follows A, D always precedes E, or C exists at all (based on a pattern usually consisting of elements A, B, C, D, and E).

It is rather with the whole and the pattern which emerges in that whole that the genre critic must be primarily concerned. A pattern is more than the summation of its parts: it includes the manner in which the parts have been used and the means by which the whole gradually unfolds, along with those often less tangible factors (authorial intent) which govern the whole process.

Genre and Source

If genre cannot be equated with form per se, neither can it be equated with content understood as subject matter or source. Obviously, the same topic may be explored in different genres. For example, people are actors in both histories and biographies as well as dramas. What distinguishes the genre is the treatment and development of the subject. Likewise, two or more authors may use a common source with different genres in mind.

The literary relationship among the gospels, especially the synoptic gospels (Matthew, Mark, and Luke), has long been recognized. This relationship is so close that it indicates "copyists" had a hand in composing them; that is, the source question includes and often revolves around attempts to establish just who is copying whom. Traditionally, the answer has been that Matthew and Luke have copied Mark plus others (Q and M or L, respectively). Although this particular thesis has recently been called into question, literary dependence remains an established fact. In the case of the Gospel According to John, no one theory of direct literary dependence has prevailed, though a similarity of source material has long been acknowledged. Largely on the basis of the material's similarity, all four of these literary works have commonly been included in the category "gospel," and each is referred to as such. While the gospel classification may be justified on a descriptive level (for reasons similar to that of Votaw's popular–historical biography and Frye's "dramatic history" classification), Norman Petersen has recently challenged it as a designation of a literary genre (particularly in the case of Matthew and Luke). After discussing the use of the noun gospel as a title designation which only occurs in Mark, Petersen notes that the evidence of authorial intent related to the theory of genre makes significant the absence of the use of this noun in Matthew and Luke.[22] He concludes that "the compositional intent as evident in what an author composed and how he composed it must take methodological precedence over the more abstract notions of kerygma or subject matter."[23] He then correctly rejects the idea that source dependence automatically means genre dependence. Explicitly, Petersen's argument suggests the possibility of removing Matthew and Luke from the gospel classification; implicitly, it challenges the view that the term automatically designates a genre.[24]

In another part of his paper, Petersen discusses "collection" as genre, and his observations there are also relevant for our present considerations. Recent scholarship has noted the possibility that collections of materials were used in constructing the gospel narratives. Matthew, for example, tends to present collected units within his narrative. Luke preserves much of the same material in a different manner, whereas, for the most part, this material is absent from Mark. On the basis of this observation, some scholars have identified the source of this collected material as a "collection" genre.[25] Similarly, Mark's gospel has been described as closely related to the aretalogy (understood as a collection of miracle stories). Petersen agrees that a collection may be thought of as a genre when groups of materials are purposefully collected in accordance with some organic principle, such as theme or character, to be presented to or maintained for a certain audience (he calls this his "WXYZ" understanding). To this extent, he affirms the research of James Robinson and, in part, that of Helmut Koester. The issue to which he addresses himself, however, is that literary point at which a collection ceases to be a collection, generically understood, and becomes something else while retaining its collected form. Accordingly, Petersen writes:

> The bridge between collection and another genre is crossed, descriptively and normatively, at that moment when an *intent* beyond the explicit claims of the component material is given either formal (structural, compositional) or material (simple editorial) expression in a text. That is to say, *a collection becomes something else at that moment when mere concatenation is replaced by composition at whatever level of sophistication.*[26]

If Petersen is correct, as it would seem he is, then a genre can be determined on the basis neither of source dependence nor of the nature of the sources. In the case of the gospels—since it has been shown by redaction criticism that the narratives are more than a concatenation—the question of genre must reside with the pattern which emerges from the whole. On any source hypothesis, gospel is not necessarily the name of the genre. The designation collection may be disqualified in view of the intentional way these writings have been compiled. The question of genre, therefore, involves an analysis of those shared conventions which comprise the pattern of the narrative and the authorial intent as it is reflected in the pattern that emerges from an analysis of the written text.

Authorial Intent

Genre criticism must admit the role of the author's intent in the construction of a literary text. This is not to deny the significance of other factors, such as the nature of the subject and even the character of the sources or traditions related to it, in the production of a generic treatise. It does mean, though, that the entire process of producing a narrative is affected by the aims, decisions, and skills of the person or persons engaged in this process. Indeed, with respect to gospel studies, the borrowing and copying of traditions is as much evidence of authorial intent as is the editorial creation of summary statements and other manifestations of the hand of the redactor. Bernard Lonergan writes:

> Heuristically, then, the context of the word is the sentence. The context of the sentence is the paragraph. The context of paragraph is the chapter. The context of the chapter is the book. The context of the book is the author's *opera omnia*, his life and times, the state of the question in his day, his problems, prospective readers, scope and aim.[27]

It is doubtful whether one can know more of an author's intentions than what can be deduced from the nature and content of his or her work.[28] For example, it is reasonable to assume that Paul "intended" to write a letter to Philemon and that an examination of its contents would reveal at least some of the reasons for his writing. Paul has stated implicitly his intentions, at least in part, by his choice of the epistolary form and by the specific concerns he addresses in the letter. The same phenomenon of objective authorial intent occurs in all literature, although its accessibility and clarity may vary from author to author and from work to work. This is so whether or not the author's identity is known. The crucial factor in determining authorial intent from the text is the sensitivity of the interpreter to the text, to hermeneutical principles, and to those disciplines which have been developed as aids for interpreting a specific text.

It is for this reason that we raise again the question of the relation-ship of form criticism to genre criticism (understood now in close proximity with redaction criticism). Petersen has stated the relation-ship:

> What we are concerned with in genre criticism in the literary sense is the criticism of literary totalities through a perception of *their* formal types and *their* laws. Form criticism and genre criticism may thus be seen as working analogously with two different classes of phenomena, the form of the parts ("Formen") and the forms (genres) of the wholes. We must insist, however, that the relationship between parts and wholes is a separate problem that may be dealt with in a variety of ways depend-ing on the nature of any given text or genre. In one case, we may have to do with a question of source relationships, in another of a relatively free authorial creation, in another of an apparently random accumulation of content.[29]

In the case of the gospels, in which there is clear evidence of literary dependence, the redaction critic's task is to identify the hand of the author and, through an analysis of those portions where it is clearly present, to determine as much as possible the author's perspective, purposes, milieu, and function. Whereas we agree with the above assessment in that we affirm the distinctiveness of each discipline and the distinctive tasks implicit therein, there is an interdependence which must not be ignored in the task of interpretation. The need for interdependence involves the paradox of what Lonergan calls the "hermeneutic circle." He writes:

> The meaning of a text is an intentional entity. It is a unity that is un-folded through parts, sections, chapters, paragraphs, sentences, words. We can grasp the unity, the whole, only through the parts. At the same time the parts are determined in their meaning by the whole which each part partially reveals. Such is the hermeneutic circle.[30]

For a theory of genre related to the gospels, all of this means that the attempt to arrive at that authorial intent which is fundamental to genre identification will involve close cooperation between form, re-daction, and genre criticisms; that is, the proper investigation of the nature of the forms and their applications by an identifiable "author" who, regardless of her or his continued anonymity, is nevertheless responsible for a unified literary entity. The paradox remains: the parts are explicable through the whole and the whole is explicable through an analysis of its parts. The system of checks which results from the cooperation of these disciplines is capable of producing reasonably reliable results for those who would inquire into the generic character of the gospels.

To summarize this brief discussion of the theory of genre, it may be said that a genre is a type of literature characterized by the formulation of a particular pattern, which employs certain literary techniques, rules, and laws. The pattern may vary, depending upon the author's purposes and the particular response the author desires from the reading audience. As such, genre transcends the notions of form and structure when these are conceived only in their external connotations. It is more than the sum of its component parts and is not limited by the character of those sources which may have been employed by the author. A genre may make use of a variety of methods, forms, themes, topics, and even collected materials in order to achieve the desired effect. Genre involves a dynamic notion of literature as preserved by a variety of cultures, and each genre must be examined within its cultural and sociological context. Finally, genre criticism is concerned with the whole and with the pattern that emerges from the total literary composition. Creativity may be seen in the author's use of the available patterns, since it is inconceivable that new patterns will emerge completely *sui generis*. The task of the genre critic, therefore, is to identify, insofar as possible, the genre of the whole in order to clarify the relationships among the parts. At the same time, the explanation of the whole will be related to an analysis of the parts. Part of this process is to identify the forces behind the generic pattern of a particular narrative, in order to understand more clearly its origin and the intent of the person or persons responsible for the whole. Basic to the entire process is the task of unraveling the intent of the author as objectified in the text, insofar as this is possible. For the gospel critic, this task will involve the disciplines of form, redaction, and genre criticism. It is on this understanding of literary genre that we will consider a literary genre with which the gospels may be identified.

A GENRE WITH WHICH THE GOSPELS MAY BE CLASSIFIED

Preliminary Considerations

As we move from a discussion of the theory of genre to a consideration of a literary genre with which the gospels may be classified, three suppositions should be stated and clarified from the outset. First, our investigation of gospel genre quite properly concerns the gospel texts as they have been preserved in their present narrative form. That is to say, the question of genre arises when the separate and, in some cases, unrelated traditions (whether oral or written, or a combination of the two) are committed to writing. In a written narrative such as the gospels, these traditions, which must originally have circulated independently of our gospels, tend to lose at least some of their characteristics as "sources" and become known only in the context of a literary whole. The question of genre emerges at precisely this point. For the manner in which a source is employed (in either a verbatim or an edited form), given a context (in the case of the gospels, the appearance of a *bios*), and committed to writing (Greek) is indicative of the intention of an author to communicate (i.e., to proclaim the "good news" as he or she understands it) to a particular audience (Greek speaking, Hellenistic, Palestinian, or non-Palestinian). On a priori grounds, therefore, we consider the question of genre to be basic to the exact interpretation of each of the gospels, for it pertains to the organization of the whole in relation to the author's intended meaning.

Second, a genre for the gospels should explain satisfactorily most of what is contained in the narratives. That is to say, it should account for the literary procedures and decisions implicit in the production of the gospels as they have been preserved; it should provide a handle by which the individual gospels may be grasped and more deeply appreciated as wholes. Further, if we seriously consider the results of other types of New Testament criticism, we must assume that the genre will admit to features not usually associated with its general characteristics: for example, as defined and identified, it must allow for the kerygma as an operative factor in the creation of the gospel narratives. In other words, as a literary entity, it must allow for the influence of a nonliterary factor, "faith," in the creation of the gospel narratives. Accordingly, the appropriate genre will both account for the whole and make ample provision for the function of the individual parts. According to our understanding of the theory of genres, therefore, it is not necessary for us to show that a particular genre accounts for *every* aspect of the gospels, only that the pattern developed therein conforms sufficiently to the generic pattern in question and that

those features present in the gospels which are not commonly associated with the characteristics of the genre do not detract so significantly
from the pattern as to require a different genre to explain them.

Third, we understand our task to be associated not only with literary criticism but also with historical research. The identification of a
relevant genre should be historically grounded on a sufficient number
of examples which indicate its literary place and function within the
ancient world. That is to say, the genre that would account for the
gospels is one which would provide meaning both for the "editor"
who employed it and for the audience to whom the narratives were
directed. In retrospect, C. W. Votaw's categories of popular–historical biography are helpful for the comparison of literary images, as are
Roland Frye's for the descriptive impact of the narratives in relation
to other later narratives.[31] Both, however, fall far short of the kind of
historical verification we deem appropriate for the identification of
a genre contemporary with and relevant to the construction of the
gospel narratives. Therefore, according to our understanding of the
theory of genres, their reconstruction based upon principles of interpretation alone—apart from clearly documentable, historical evidence
related to the "author's" time and milieu—is, for the purposes of the
present research, excluded from consideration. We are clearly look-
ing for genres contemporary with the evangelists, in order to identify
both the nearest parallels and the literary process which adequately
explains the generic pattern.

Evidence for an Appropriate Genre

There are two important observations about the nature of the gospel narratives which can assist in the quest for a suitable genre. The
first is basic: the gospels are related to the person of Jesus. I referred
to this trait earlier as the *bios* factor, a term intended to denote that
the traditions directly attributed to Jesus have been preserved in the
gospels in a way and context that give emphasis not only to the
traditions themselves but even more to the person around whom they
were formulated. This aspect of the gospels directs our attention to
genres of a biographical nature current at the time the canonical
gospels were written. The second observation, which may eliminate
some of the generic options, is simply that the gospels were apparently not primarily conceived for the purpose of conveying historical

information. This is not to say that one who examines the gospels is not concerned with history, or that it is not possible to glean reliable historical information through a very careful examination of the texts. In fact, the portraits the evangelists sketch may be more accurate than our summaries and reconstructions would indicate. But the predominant interest of the text is not to comply with the canons of historiography (ancient or modern). These observations combine to provide important insight for the search for a gospel genre: the evangelists have presented traditions related to Jesus in a literary narrative about Jesus which was not designed with the *intention* of conforming to the standards of historiography, even ancient historiography.

One of the chief obstacles to solving the problem of the genre of the gospels is the apparent lack of a type with which they may be classified as literary wholes. It is true that, on the surface, no literary type projects itself unmistakably. Although there is no form critical evidence that the evangelists adhered to an obvious generic type, there is sufficient evidence of a literary type which could have contributed a great deal (from a literary point of view) to the basic format the gospel writers appropriated for their own proclamations. The evidence to which we refer exists in a type of *bios* literature, the primary purpose of which was to praise, a body of *bios* literature whose characteristics, because of this primary concern, may be examined through its rhetorical roots—*epideictic oratory* and, more specifically, the *encomium*. This type of literature is suggested by our observations on the nature of the gospels, for this body of literature also has as its subject a significant and accomplished person who is not portrayed primarily through historiographical methodology—Jesus. Evidence for this type of literature is implicit in the discussions of the differences between ancient history and ancient biography.

Polybius (second century B.C.) is perhaps the earliest author to make the clear distinction between history and biography. In *The Histories,* when he comes to the point of discussing the achievements of Philopoemen, he digresses briefly to explain his literary procedure. He notes first the importance of narrating the exploits and character of eminent men, affirming the worthiness of such a topic in comparison with accounts of "lifeless buildings" and cities. Next, he explains that he had previously composed an extensive, separate account of the life of Philopoemen, which includes his education, family, and achievements. In his current history, Polybius omitted most of the details from his earlier account, presenting instead only a brief summary of his subject's accomplishments. The essential difference between the two narratives is described in the following:

> For just as the former work, being in the form of an encomium, demanded a summary and somewhat exaggerated account of his achievements, so the present history, which distributes praise and blame impartially, demands a strictly true account and one which states the ground on which either praise or blame is based. (X. 21. 8)[32]

The contrast is obvious: history, which distributes praise and blame impartially "demands a strictly true account," clearly establishing the ground on which praise or blame is based. *Encomium* (a form of biographical narrative), on the other hand, demands a "somewhat exaggerated account of . . . achievements," in which the author may praise at will.

In his *Epistulae ad Familiares*, Cicero (first century B.C.) requests a favor of a friend. Aware that Lucius Lucceius was writing a history of Rome which would include the period of his own contributions, Cicero asks Lucceius to write about him as a figure of great importance. He is aware that such a request would necessitate a digression from the purposes of the historical narrative. Setting modesty aside, however, Cicero boldly describes the kind of narrative he is soliciting:

> So I frankly ask you again and again to eulogize my actions with even more warmth than perhaps you feel, and in that respect to disregard the canons of history; and . . . if you find that such personal partiality enhances my merits even to exaggeration in your eyes, I ask you not to disdain it, and of your bounty to bestow on our love even a little more than may be allowed by truth. (V. xii. 3)[33]

Like Polybius a century earlier, Cicero bears witness to history which does not admit exaggeration and to a type of *bios* narrative which freely provides for the bestowal of "love even a little more than may be allowed by truth."

In the second century A.D., Lucian wrote a polemical treatise, *How to Write History*, composed as an invective against those misusing the discipline of history in their descriptions of the Parthian War. Again, the contrast is between history and encomium; and, as might be expected, the latter does not fare well in comparison with the former (*History* 7):

> To begin with, let us look at this for a serious fault: most of them neglect to record the events and spend their time lauding rulers and generals, extolling their own to the skies and slandering the enemy's beyond all reserve; they do not realise that the dividing line and frontier between history and encomium is not a narrow isthmus but rather a mighty wall: . . . if indeed the encomiast's sole concern is to praise and please in any way he can the one he praises, and if he can achieve his aim by lying, little will he care! But history cannot admit a lie, even a tiny one, any more than the windpipe, as sons of doctors say, can tolerate anything entering it in swallowing.[34]

Without belaboring the point, it is apparent that Lucian's distinction, though asserted through invective, is identical to that of both Polybius and Cicero.

A contemporary of Cicero was Cornelius Nepos, who, as far as we know, was the first to organize his "Lives" in parallel form. In this respect, he may be considered the forerunner to Plutarch. In a preface to his life of *Pelopidas*, Cornelius Nepos states his literary problem and provides us with his procedural solution:

> Pelopidas, the Theban, is better known to historians than to the general public. I am in doubt how to give an account of his merits; for I fear that if I undertake to tell of his deeds, I shall seem to be writing a history rather than a biography; but if I merely touch upon the high points, I am afraid that to those unfamiliar with Grecian literature it will not be perfectly clear how great a man he was. Therefore I shall meet both difficulties as well as I can having regard both for the weariness and the lack of information of my readers. (XVI. 1. 1)[35]

The dichotomy now is between history and biography, that is, *vita*. It occurs almost as an apology, for, whereas Cornelius Nepos states his primary task is to relate simply the merits and greatness of his subject, Pelopidas's obscurity would seem to demand that he be treated more extensively.

Finally, Plutarch (late first century A.D.) refers to the problem in his parallel lives—more specifically, in his introduction to the lives of *Alexander and Caesar*:

> It is the life of Alexander the king, and of Caesar, who overthrew Pompey, that I am writing in this book, and the multitude of the deeds to be

treated is so great that I shall make no other preface than to entreat my readers, in case I do not tell of all the famous actions of these men, nor even speak exhaustively at all in each particular case, but in epitome for the most part, not to complain. For it is not histories that I am writing, but lives; and in the most illustrious deeds there is not always a manifestation of the virtue or vice, nay, a slight thing like a phrase or a jest often makes a greater revelation of character than battles where thousands fall, or the greatest armaments, or siege of cities. Accordingly, just as painters get the likenesses in their portraits from the face and the expression of the eyes, wherein the character shows itself, but make very little account of the other parts of the body, so I must be permitted to devote myself rather to the signs of the soul in men, and by means of these to portray the life of each, leaving to others the descriptions of their great contests. (I. 1–3)[36]

The manner in which the dichotomy evolves is significant. Plutarch speaks of history which is concerned with all the actions, battles, armaments, and sieges of cities. Conversely, he is engaged in producing *bioi* which seek to capture an epitome, the character, or such "signs of the soul" as may be reflected more acutely in a mere phrase or jest by his subject. His interest is in producing a portrait of the person rather than a detailed description of every aspect of his life or even every great contest or battle in which the hero was engaged. Consequently, to suit his peculiar purposes, history is discounted in favor of a biographical alternative he calls *bioi*.

At this point, several observations should be made about the dichotomy implicit in the above references. The distinction is consistently upheld in each case. When one realizes that four centuries are spanned by these authors, the distinction between history and biography is even more convincing. The examples cited represent both Greek and Roman authors, with diverse intentions: the appreciative history of Polybius, the "humble" request of Cicero, the invective of Lucian, the explanation of Cornelius Nepos, and the clarification of Plutarch; but the continuity is remarkable and the distinction appears to be representative, in general, of the ancient world.

From our contemporary perspective, it will be noted that the literary objective in each case is based upon a distinctive claim about historical truth. This means that, according to the classical writers, the truth contained in history demands the proper and faithful recording of events, along with accurate reports about the chief actors in them. The truth of biography, on the other hand, aims at making the proper assessment of a person and her or his character, in accordance with the intentions of the particular author and the availability and nature of the traditions relevant to the literary portrait.[37] Thus the responsible historian could not admit a lie, whereas the biographer might either resort to exaggeration or limit the scope of his or her material so as to exclude those aspects that do not reveal character in order to affirm both the significance and the model nature which made the portrait worthy of attention. It is clear, therefore, that, given the dichotomy, the hermeneutical principles employed in the examination of any literary text of the period will depend upon the type of text under investigation, especially where history and biography are concerned.

It follows that these authors are referring to methodology as well as to individual kinds of narratives. History, for example, must not be limited to such grandiose projects as Polybius's history or Lucceius's history of Rome. History also embraces less ambitious attempts to recount past battles, single events, or the actions of generals in war —oratorical attempts with which Lucian was primarily concerned. These authors had the history genre in mind as well as the methodological principles by which books or treatises classified under this genre are produced. Furthermore, there appears to be a consensus concerning the nomenclature related to the genre. Works may vary in topic, scope, and, to some extent, purpose, but the term *history* is applicable in each case, and each author appears to understand its designation, although each may differ over the specific content of history.

Likewise, one cannot place arbitrarily restrictive definitions upon the type of biography to which these authors refer. For example, one cannot limit the definition of the *encomium* to the formal literary exercises common to secondary education of the Greco–Roman period. Nor should one be overly restrictive in one's understanding of *bios* literature of that period. Biographical literature, in contrast with history, is also indicative of a literary type distinguished by particular methodological presuppositions. It is precisely at this point, though, that we must recognize that, unlike historical literature which could be and was classified as history, there is no single umbrella which could cover the many biographical treatises. Thus we have arrived at perhaps the most perplexing point in the question of the generic understanding of the gospels: New Testament scholars feel relatively comfortable with the reference to Luke as a "historian," even in a general classical sense, but they continue to sift through the more limited types of Hellenistic biographical compositions in search of a genre broad enough to include the gospels. Finding none which fits precisely, they then tend to exclude altogether the possibility of any affinity with ancient biography. It is likely that the ancients themselves had similar problems with their own biographical literature. Consider, for example, the dichotomy between history and biography. In each example cited, "history" is the standard form, which is compared and contrasted (methodologically speaking) with another kind of literature. In the cases of Polybius, Cicero, and Lucian, the biographical reference, either direct or indirect, is to *encomium*. Cornelius Nepos and Plutarch refer to *vitae* and *bioi*, respectively. It is unlikely, however, that this different terminology indicates separate genres and different methodological presuppositions.

Polybius describes the encomium as a "somewhat exaggerated account of his achievements"; Cicero asks his friend to "eulogize [his] actions" in a way that "enhances [his] merits even to exaggeration"; while Lucian complains that "most of them neglect to record the events and spend their time lauding rulers and generals, extolling their own to the skies and slandering the enemy's beyond all reserve." Common to each of these characterizations is the portrayal of greatness and merit, and it is this literary objective which may cause an author to dispense with the canons of history, either by exaggeration (amplification) or by selection. The use of the term *encomium* is appropriate, for it represents rhetorical justification for such a literary procedure. The encomium was a literary exercise common in Greco–Roman education, designed to train the student in literary portraiture, the necessary *topoi* and techniques being prescribed by the rhetoricians. There may be common themes in history and biography (such as birth, education, events, achievements, death, things which happen after death), but history assigns praise or blame impartially whereas the encomium utilizes the same themes, drawing freely upon comparison and amplification, in order to make a case for the merits of the literary subject.[38]

In using the terms *vita* and *bios*, do Cornelius Nepos and Plutarch have in mind a different task? As we have noted previously in the case of *Pelopidas* (p. 39), the dilemma to which Cornelius Nepos addresses himself does not seem radically different from the agenda of Polybius, Cicero, and Lucian:

> I am in doubt how to give an account of his merits; for I fear that if I undertake to tell of his deeds, I shall seem to be writing a history rather than a biography; but if I merely touch upon the high points, I am afraid that to those unfamiliar with Grecian literature it will not be perfectly clear how great a man he was. (XVI. 1. 1)

As he himself states, Cornelius Nepos was interested in building a case for greatness. Plutarch admittedly presents a more complicated situation, but he does admit to selection and amplification, even to the point of preferring a phrase or a jest to build his literary protrait.

Closely related to this observation is D. L. Clark's suggestion that the rhetorical device known as *comparison* may be the key to the format of Plutarch's parallel lives.[39] There is evidence in Plutarch's Lives to demonstrate the impact of the encomium upon his work, as far as *topoi* and techniques are concerned, but it is equally clear that Plutarch has not dispensed entirely with the canons of history writing (see, for example, *Theseus* I. 3). In spite of the complexity of both Plutarch and Cornelius Nepos, the literary conventions and authorial intentions indicate that there is not a major generic difference in the biographical type presented by each of the five authors mentioned thus far.

For additional evidence on the existence of a genre of laudatory biography, we move from the dichotomy between history and biography to other passages which reflect the intentions of specific authors. For now, it is important to note only the common denominator in each passage which indicates the intent to praise and to demonstrate the greatness of the person in whose honor the narrative has been written. For example, Xenophon writes in *Agesilaus*:

> I know how difficult it is to write an appreciation of Agesilaus that shall be worthy of his virtue and glory. Nevertheless, the attempt must be made. For it would not be seemly that so good a man, just because of his perfection, should receive no tributes of praise, however inadequate. (I. 1)[40]

Here the objective, "an appreciation . . . worthy of his virtue and glory," is consistent with another literary model with a similar generic pattern, Isocrates' *Evagoras*. Isocrates' intention is represented in *Evagoras* 1–4:

> . . . I judged that Evagoras (if the dead have any perception of that which takes place in this world), while gladly accepting these offerings and rejoicing in the spectacle of your devotion and princely magnificence in honouring him, would feel far greater gratitude to anyone who could worthily recount his principles in life and his perilous deeds than to all other men; for we shall find that men of ambition and greatness of soul not only are desirous of praise for such things, but prefer a glorious death to life, zealously seeking glory rather than existence, and doing all that lies in their power to leave behind a memory of themselves that shall never die. . . . But the spoken words which should adequately recount the deeds of Evagoras would make his virtues never to be forgotten among all mankind.[41]

Again, the object is praise, and the effect of the "spoken words" (that is, the encomium he is writing) is the preservation for posterity of Evagoras's greatness.

Philo states very clearly what he is attempting to accomplish in his *De vita Mosis*:

> I purpose to write the life of Moses, whom some describe as legislator of the Jews, others as the interpreter of the Holy Laws. I hope to bring the story of this greatest and most perfect of men to the knowledge of such as deserve not to remain in ignorance of it; . . . Greek men of letters have refused to treat him as worthy of memory, possibly through envy, and also because in many cases the ordinances of the legislators of the different states are opposed to his. . . . But I will disregard their malice, and tell the story of Moses as I have learned it, both from the sacred books, the wonderful monuments of his wisdom which he has left behind him, and from some of the elders of the nation; for I always interwove what I was told with what I read, and thus believed myself to have a closer knowledge than others of his life's history. (1–2, 4)[42]

With equally high ambition, Lucian would preserve the memory of Demonax as a model for aspiring philosophers:

> It was on the cards, it seems, that our modern world should not be altogether destitute of noteworthy and memorable men, but should produce enormous physical prowess and a highly philosophic mind. I speak with reference to . . . Heracles and . . . especially to Demonax, the philosopher. . . . It is now fitting to tell of Demonax for two reasons— that he may be retained in memory by men of culture as far as I can bring it about, and that young men of good instincts who aspire to

philosophy may not have to shape themselves by ancient precedents alone, but may be able to set themselves a pattern from our modern world and to copy that man, the best of all the philosophers whom I know about. (I. 1–2, 4)[43]

Tacitus appears to have similar purposes in writing his *Agricola*. Notice his concluding statements:

Whatever we have loved in Agricola, whatever we have admired, abides, and will abide, in the hearts of men, in the procession of the ages, in the records of history. Many of the ancients has Forgetfulness engulfed as though fame nor name were theirs. Agricola, whose story here is told, will outlive death, to be our children's heritage. (46)[44]

In each of the examples offered, the stated purpose is essentially to build a case for praising the subject of the treatise, because his life is considered by each author to be worthy of attention and emulation for an immediate audience. Accordingly, these works belong to the type of biography so frequently contrasted with history by the ancients.

What we have attempted to demonstrate, first by reference to the classical dichotomy between history and biography, and, second, by reference to passages specifying authorial intent, is that there did exist a type of literature whose primary concern was to show individual greatness and merit. There is ample evidence that such a genre existed. Judging from the character of the testimonies cited, this body of literature must have been both extensive and diverse; but, regrettably, it does not carry one single nomenclature. At times, these treatises were appropriate for delivery at games and festivals; at other times, they were appropriate at funeral celebrations, and at still others, in legislative assembly settings, where there was an emphasis on personal defense or vindication. Regardless of the occasion, the primary purpose was to praise and demonstrate praiseworthiness. For the present, we may be satisfied with the designation "laudatory biography."

Description and Definition

Now that its existence is established, the need arises for a more precise description and definition of the laudatory biography genre. It may be described tentatively as an account which resembles a portrait by a painter (Plutarch's analogy), one which is concerned not so much with every detail but is devoted rather to the communication of the impression desired by the artist. Such an account is more than a repetition of facts, events, achievements, or virtue alone, though it may involve any or all of these. Some such treatises admittedly exaggerate the truth (Polybius, Cicero), some even to the point of lying (Cicero, Lucian). While some of these works which specifically bear the title *bios* or *vita* appear to be preoccupied with character (Plutarch), and at least some are designed to entertain, they are all, in one way or another, concerned with greatness and, implicitly if not explicitly, the praiseworthiness of the central figure.

Fortunately, we need not rely solely upon such scattered references for a proper understanding of this genre. Because the encomium has been specifically mentioned in contrast with history, and because of its recognized role in the development of biography,[45] an examination of this rhetorical device will reveal something of the nature of the laudatory biography. There are rhetorical discussions of the encomium which delineate its characteristics, and we may begin by examining these literary principles. The writing of encomia was codified within the educational system from which came the practitioners who continued to develop this popular laudatory type.[46] A word of caution must accompany this procedure, for the undertaking is made solely to elucidate the genre under discussion and should not be understood as equating questions of genre with those secondary "how-to-write" questions so vital to one's educational development. We are not trying to claim that there are direct affinities between the gospels and the encomium per se; nor, for that matter, are we arguing that the evangelists were writing with a textbook on rhetoric before them, thereby producing something resembling a so-called biographical encomium.[47] We are primarily concerned with identifying the *topoi* and techniques commonly associated with what we have referred to as laudatory biography. The procedure is valid only insofar as the specific rules and techniques—of which the usage in the genre depended on the writer's purpose—are helpful in understanding that genre whose existence is verified by the testimonies of those cited above.[48]

The encomium is a literary form whose development and popularity can be traced over more than five centuries from the testimonies of rhetoricians as well as from the literary examples which have been preserved. One of the earliest rhetorical works to include a discussion of the encomium was the *Rhetorica* of Aristotle (fourth century B.C.). Aristotle stresses the basis on which praise and censure are awarded (the concepts of virtue and vice) and outlines the techniques of amplification and comparison (*Rh.*, I. 6. 9). *Rhetorica ad Alexandrum* is a second rhetorical work which has been preserved under the authorship of Aristotle. The authorship has, however, been disputed, even though its rules for encomium writing (*Rh. Al.*, III–IV) approximate those of Aristotle. The date is fixed at the beginning of the third century B.C. These two works are followed by *Rhetorica ad Herennium,* often attributed to Cicero, written circa the first century B.C. Cicero (first century B.C.) also wrote the treatise *De Partitione Oratoria,* the one in which he devotes considerable attention to the art of encomium writing (XXI). Two additional authors should be mentioned for their rhetorical works: Theon of Smyrna (second century A.D.) and Hermogenes of Tarsus (second century A.D.).

The history of the form cannot be circumscribed by the dates of the rhetoricians. Apparently, the encomium was a poetic device before its prose counterpart developed. Isocrates, who extols prose over poetry, gives himself credit for transferring the poetic encomium into a prose format. This is a questionable assertion[49] (perhaps an example of the encomiast's interest in "first" credits; see Quintilian, *Institutio oratoria* III. 7. 10–18, on pp. 53–54), but it is interesting to note Isocrates' comments that poets "can represent the gods as associating with men, conversing with and aiding in battle whomever they please"; "can treat of these subjects not only in conventional expressions, but in words now exotic, now newly coined, and now in figures of speech, neglecting none, but using every kind with which to embroider their poetry"; and can make use of "metre and rhythm" (*Evagoras* 8–11). By contrast, orators are not permitted such literary luxuries: "they must use with precision only words in current use and only such ideas as bear upon the actual facts," although Isocrates admits elsewhere that the orator may use extravagant language (*Busiris* 4). However accurate Isocrates' claims to original composition, his references do testify to the prevalence of the encomium as a poetic form in antiquity. Exactly when and how the form was adapted to prose cannot be determined precisely, but it is clear (and here, too, Isocrates is a good example) that the transition was made without diminishing its popularity.

In the rhetorical schools, there were three common divisions of rhetoric: deliberative, forensic, and epideictic.[50] The encomium is included under the third of these divisions, said by W. C. Wright to have originated with Gorgias.[51] In several rhetorical works, this division is referred to as "encomiasticon" rather than "epideictic,"[52] which probably only emphasizes the important characteristics of the third division and its more commonly applied function, that of praise. Consistent with the practical emphases of rhetorical education, the threefold division is largely based upon the purposes and occasions for which the speeches were prepared. Aristotle, for example, states that the "deliberative" speech may be either hortatory or dissuasive, "for both those who give advice in private and those who speak in the assembly invariably either exhort or dissuade" (*Rh*. I. 3. 3), a purpose which indicates a legislative setting. The "forensic" speech may be either accusatory or defensive, "for litigants must necessarily either accuse or defend" (I. 3. 3), a purpose consonant with judicial deliberation. The epideictic speech "has for its subject praise or blame" (I. 3. 3), a catchall category for use in celebrative, ceremonial, official, or extraofficial settings which do not require legislative or judicial actions.[53] The functional and practical basis for these divisions means there may be considerable interactions, since common conventions may be used for different purposes:

> All the species of oratory have now been distinguished. They are to be employed both separately, when suitable, and jointly, with a combination of their qualities—for though they have very considerable differences, yet in their practical application they overlap. In fact the same is true of them as of the various species of human beings; these also are partly alike and partly different in their appearances and in their perceptions. (*Rh. Al.* 1427b. 30–35; see also *Rh.* I. 9. 35–36)[54]

Quintilian also notes:

> All other *species* fall under these three *genera*: you will not find one in which we have not to praise or blame, to advise or dissuade, to drive home or refute a charge, while conciliation, narration, proof, exaggeration, extenuation, and the moulding of the minds of the audience by exciting or allaying their passions, are common to all three kinds of oratory. I cannot even agree with those who hold that *laudatory* subjects are concerned with the question of what is honourable, *deliberative* with the question of what is expedient, and *forensic* with the question of what is just: the division made is easy and neat rather than true: for all three kinds rely on the mutual assistance of the other. (*Inst.* III. 4. 15–16)[55]

In this regard, it is interesting to note that Origen, an early Christian father, specifically refers to encomia with reference to what Jesus chose not to do in self-defense before Pilate (*Contra Celsum*, Preface 1–2). Origen's usage not only demonstrates that there is interaction among the rhetorical divisions but also that at least one early Christian was familiar with the technical use of this rhetorical term by the beginning of the third century A.D.

Bearing in mind this interdependence of the three divisions of oratory, the essential purpose of the epideictic division is to praise or censure. Aristotle defines the term concisely: "The epideictic kind has for its subject praise or blame" (*Rh.* I. 3. 3), and Cicero emphasizes its importance by referring to it as "the nurse of that orator whom we wish to delineate and about whom we design to speak more particularly" (*Orator* XI. 37). The encomium, an important part of the epideictic division, was particularly concerned with praise. Although it had its distinctive characteristics, it also used literary techniques common to the whole division. Two of these should be especially noted, for they are common in the laudatory biographical genre as well as in encomia: *amplification* and *comparison*. *Amplification* as a technique was encountered in connection with the testimonies of the history–biography dichotomy, though it was not then isolated for discussion. It was present in Polybius's statement in which the encomium was referred to as a form comprising "a summary and somewhat exaggerated account." Cicero appears to request amplification in the form of exaggeration: "to bestow on our love even a little more than may be allowed by truth." Lucian sees such exaggeration as tantamount to lying. In Plutarch, it is evident in a slightly different way, namely, the projected emphasis upon and amplification of something as seemingly insignificant as a mere phrase or jest. In each case, a literary technique common to the epideictic is involved. In fact, within the division itself the technique may work for both praise and blame.

> The eulogistic species of oratory consists, to put it briefly, in the amplification of creditable purposes and actions and speeches and attribution of qualities that do not exist, while the vituperative species is the opposite, the minimization of creditable qualities and the amplification of discreditable ones. (*Rh. Al.* 1425b. 35)[56]

Two references in Aristotle's *Rhetorica* indicate the extent to which this technique was used: "for we should praise even a man who had

not achieved anything, if we felt confident that he was likely to do so"
(I. 9. 33) and "even if a man has not actually done a given good thing,
we shall bestow *praise* on him, if we are sure that he is the sort of
man who *would* do it" (I. 9. 5; see also 25–30).

If amplification meant accenting positive attributes, it also meant
minimizing the negative to the point of omission. In *De Partitione
Oratoria* XXII, Cicero specifically refers to the omission of negative
qualities. This reference involves a brief statement of the use of a
person's family in an encomium: "This must be praised briefly and
with moderation, or if it is disgraceful, or if of low station, either
passed over or so treated as to increase the glory of the person you are
praising . . . ." The same procedure was applicable to other *topoi*.[57]
Although difficult to document, two examples have been noted. In his
Politica (1311b) Aristotle states that Evagoras was murdered, "but
Isocrates is silent with respect to the manner of the death of his hero
Evagoras."[58] Since the manner of death is important for the encomiast,
it is difficult to understand why Isocrates omits such a reference in his
Evagoras unless for the reasons offered above by Cicero. Stuart has
documented the second example.[59] In the *Hellenica*, Xenophon tells
how Agesilaus's "stiff knee . . . might have altered the course of
history." But there is no reference to it in his *Agesilaus*; nor, indeed,
is there a sketch of Agesilaus's personal appearance.[60] In practice,
therefore, *amplification* and its opposite, *minimization* and, in some
cases, *omission*, were common in epideictic oratory; and Stuart has
vividly captured the orator's purpose: "His business was to magnify,
not to dissect."[61]

Comparison was also germane to epideictic oratory. This technique
consisted of a comparison of the central character with another person
to illustrate how the former excelled over the latter. Aristotle, in his
Rhetorica ad Alexandrum, tends to prefer comparison of the central
character to a person of obviously lesser accomplishment.

> A third way is to set in comparison with the thing you are saying the
> smallest of the things that fall into the same class, for thus your case will
> appear magnified, just as men of medium height appear taller when
> standing by the side of men shorter than themselves. (1426a. 25–30)

So, for example, in *Agesilaus*, Xenophon describes some of the weaknesses of the "Persian king," in comparison with whom Agesilaus
possessed far greater qualities (*Agesilaus* VIII–IX). Aristotle, on the

other hand, prefers to compare two individuals of approximately equal rank, thereby demonstrating how the subject chosen for praise surpasses another great figure.

> The comparison should be with famous men; that will strengthen your case; it is a noble thing to surpass men who are themselves great. It is only natural that methods of "heightening the effect" should be attached particularly to speeches of praise; they aim at proving superiority over others, and any such superiority is a form of nobleness. Hence if you cannot compare your hero with famous men, you should at least compare him with other people generally, since any superiority is held to reveal excellence. (*Rh.* I. 9. 20–25)

Consider, for example, how Isocrates' assertion of Helen's beauty and attraction is enhanced by the status of her suitors (chief among whom is Theseus). Or consider how, immediately preceding Agricola's victory in Britain, Tacitus uses the speech of Calgacus, which reflects the quality of the opposition, in order to illustrate Agricola's skill both as an orator and as a military general. (*Agricola* 29–30)

Comparisons do not need to be direct but may be implied in more general statements:

> In view of these facts, if any of the poets have used extravagant expressions in characterizing any man of the past, asserting that he was a god among men, or a mortal divinity, all praise of that kind would be especially in harmony with the noble qualities of Evagoras. (*Evagoras* 72)

> Justly may the man be counted blessed who was in love with glory from early youth and won more of it than any man of his age; who, being by nature very covetous of honour, never once knew defeat from the day that he became a king; who, after living to the utmost limit of human life, died without one blunder to his account, either concerning the men he led or in dealing with those on whom he made war. (*Agesilaus* X. 4)

Comparison, therefore, may be considered, along with *amplification*, as an important technique of encomium writing.

Having examined briefly two techniques characteristic of epideictic literature and frequently encountered in encomia, the next step in the description of laudatory biography is to identify more precisely the particular occasions, subjects, and *topoi* with which the encomium is primarily concerned. The encomium, already identified as one of the more important types of epideictic oratory, may be described as a form of display or public oration. As such, it served as an elementary exercise fundamental to the educational systems throughout the Greco-Roman world because of its relevance for all aspects of public life.[62] As previously noted, its several purposes include entertaining the audience, and for this reason it was particularly relevant for all types of festive occasions, such as public games. Encomia were commonly delivered at victory celebrations held either in honor of victorious athletes or in celebration of returning conquerors. Even the funeral, viewed as an opportunity to celebrate the illustrious deeds and accomplishments of the deceased, could occasion the commissioning of an encomium, which would closely resemble a funeral oration.[63]

Generally speaking, almost any subject could lend itself to encomiastic treatment. Polybius has noted that cities were honored with encomia. Quintilian recognizes that a variety of subject matter was possible, although the praise of gods and men was most common: "This form of oratory is directed in the main to the praise of gods and men, but may occasionally be applied to the praise of animals or even inanimate objects" (*Inst.* III. 7. 6). Isocrates' *Helen* contains references to encomia praising "bumble-bees, and salt and kindred topics" (*Helen* 13; for salt, see also Plato, *Symposium* 177b). Certainly, Lucian's "The Fly" is a classic example of, perhaps even a model for, the comic use of the encomium. In addition, the treatment of Helen of Troy by both Gorgias and Isocrates shows how a work which is ostensibly a treatment of a personage can actually be concerned with a mythological figure (see also Isocrates' treatment of Busiris). These illustrations show the variety of subjects which could be and were treated in encomia. At times, one can see interaction of praiseworthy subjects, for example, a man of greatness may derive honor from the character of the city in which he was born; conversely, a city may derive additional greatness from the heroes nurtured within its walls. For example, in Plutarch's parallel lives of Theseus and Romulus, the founders of Athens and Rome, respectively (*Theseus* II. 1), the subjects' honor is enhanced by the subsequent greatness of the cities they founded. Likewise, the stature attained by the cities may be attributed to the character of their founders. Consequently, Plutarch's treatment is a tribute both to founders and cities.

The subject having been chosen, topics and procedures were readily available to the encomiast for the accomplishment of his particular literary purposes. Quintilian has codified one such set of rules.[64] The text will be quoted extensively, to give the reader a better idea of the numerous possibilities and a fuller appreciation of one rhetorician's understanding of the requirements for an encomium of a person written in the first century A.D.

There is greater variety required in the praise of men. In the first place there is a distinction to be made as regards time between the period in which the objects of our praise lived and the time preceding their birth; and further, in the case of the dead we must also distinguish the period following their death. With regard to things preceding a man's birth, there are his country, his parents and ancestors, a theme which may be handled in two ways. For either it will be creditable to the objects of our praise not to have fallen short of the fair fame of their country and of their sires or to have ennobled a humble origin by the glory of their achievements. Other topics to be drawn from the period preceding their birth will have reference to omens or prophecies foretelling their future greatness, such as the oracle which is said to have foretold that the son of Thetis would be greater than his father. The praise of the individual himself will be based on his character, his physical endowments and external circumstances. Physical and accidental advantages provide a comparatively unimportant theme, which requires variety of treatment. At times for instance we extol beauty and strength in honorific terms, as Homer does in the case of Agamemnon and Achilles; at times again weakness may contribute largely to our admiration, as when Homer says that Tydeus was small of stature but a good fighter. Fortune too may confer dignity as in the case of kings and princes (for they have a fairer field for the display of their excellences) but on the other hand the glory of good deeds may be enhanced by the smallness of their resources. Moreover the praise awarded to external and accidental advantages is given, not to their possession, but to their honourable employment. For wealth and power and influence, since they are the sources of strength, are the surest test of character for good or evil; they make us better or they make us worse. Praise awarded to character is always just, but may be given in various ways. It has sometimes proved the more effective course to trace a man's life and deeds in due chronological order, praising his natural gifts as a child, then his progress at school, and finally the whole course of his life, including words as well as deeds. At times on the other hand it is well to divide our praises, dealing separately with the various virtues, fortitude, justice, self-control and the rest of them and to assign to each virtue the deeds performed under its influence. We shall have to decide which of these two methods will be the more serviceable, according to the nature of the subject; but we must bear in mind the fact that what most pleases an audience is the celebration of deeds which our hero was the first or only man or at any rate one of the very few to perform: and to these we must add any other achievements which surpassed hope or expectation, emphasizing what was done for the sake of others rather than what he performed on his own behalf. It is not always possible to deal with the time subsequent to our hero's death: this is due not merely to the fact that we sometimes praise him, while still alive, but also that there are but few occasions when we have a chance to celebrate the award of divine honours, posthumous votes of thanks, or statues erected at the public expense. Among such themes of panegyric I would mention monuments of genius that have stood the test of time. For some great men like Menander have received ampler justice from the verdict of posterity than from their own age. Children reflect glory on their parents, cities on their founders, laws on those who made them, arts on their inventors and institutions on those that first introduced them; for instance Numa first laid down rules for the worship of the gods, and Publicola first ordered that the lictor's rods should be lowered in salutation to the people. (*Inst.* III. 7. 10–18)

Then there are the rules of Hermogenes, circa 150 A.D., essentially the same as those of Quintilian, although presented differently. For the sake of brevity, we include only those rules related to encomia of men.

Topics for encomia of a man are his race; . . . . his city; . . . . his family. . . . You will say what marvelous things befell at his birth, as dreams or signs or the like. Next his nurture. . . . Then training, how he was trained and educated. Not only so, but the nature of the soul and body will be set forth, and of each under these heads: for the body—beauty, stature, agility, might; for the soul—justice, self-control, wisdom, manliness. Next his pursuits, what sort of life he led—that of philosopher, orator, or soldier, and most properly his deeds, for deeds come under the head of pursuits. . . . Then external resources, such as kin, friends, possessions, household fortune, etc. Then time, how long he lived, much or little, for either gives rise to encomia. . . . Then, too, from the manner of his end, as that he died fighting for his fatherland, and, if there were anything extraordinary under that head. . . . You will draw praise also from the one who slew him. . . . You will describe also what was done after his end, whether funeral games were ordained in his honour; . . . whether there was an oracle concerning his bones; . . . whether his children were famous. . . . But the greatest opportunity in encomia is through comparisons, which you will draw as the occasion may suggest.[65]

H. I. Marrou's outline of the system of Theon (114–140 A.D.) is of considerable interest as an example of the minute details which some rhetoricians used in their discussions of *topoi*:

Suppose a certain person, living or dead, real or mythical, is to be eulogised. According to the theory, there will be thirty-six definite stages, divided and subdivided as follows:

I. *Exterior Excellences*

  (a) Noble birth

  (b) Environment

      1. Native city
      2. Fellow citizens
      3. Excellence of the city's political regime
      4. Parents and family

  (c) Personal advantages

      1. Education
      2. Friends
      3. Fame
      4. Public service
      5. Wealth
      6. Children, number and beauty of
      7. Happy death

II. *Bodily Excellences*

      1. Health
      2. Strength
      3. Beauty
      4. Bubbly vitality and capacity for deep feeling

III. *Spiritual Excellences*

  (a) Virtues

      1. Wisdom
      2. Temperance
      3. Courage
      4. Justice
      5. Piety
      6. Nobility
      7. Sense of greatness

  (b) Resultant Actions

    (A) As to their objectives:

      1. Altruistic and disinterested
      2. Good, not utilitarian or pleasant
      3. In the public interest
      4. Braving risks and dangers

    (B) As to their circumstances:

      1. Timely
      2. Original

3. Performed alone
4. More than anyone else?
5. Few to help him?
6. Old head on young shoulders?
7. Against all the odds
8. At great cost to himself
9. Prompt and efficient.

All this was absolutely basic, and other sections might be added—how highly eminent men had thought of him; all the striking deeds he would undoubtedly have done if he had not unfortunately died. . . .[66]

In Marrou's discussion of the encomium, the rigidity of the system and the multiplicity of themes are emphasized as the above summary-in-outline illustrates; and Marrou argues that the educational system demanded strict conformity with the form. Whereas this may have been true in the schoolroom, this observation must be modified by the previous statement of Quintilian ("according to the nature of the subject") and by the fact that none of the models which have been preserved conforms to these criteria without considerable variation. Some of the variations may be accounted for by the fact that not every school advocated the same rules and topics, as is obvious from a cursory reading of the rhetoricians listed above. Nor could every category apply to every individual: what is relevant to the soldier, for example, is not necessarily important for the orator, and what is important for the philosopher might differ from that which is praiseworthy for soldier, statesman, or orator. Variation can also be expected in technique, even when the subject of two different encomia is the same (as in the treatments of Helen of Troy by Gorgias and Isocrates). The variables, therefore, are numerous; and the decision involved in the composition of an encomium depends, in the final analysis, upon the nature of the subject, the purposes of the author, and the occasion for which the encomium is composed.

SUMMARY

Turning again to the description of that laudatory biography evidenced by the works of Polybius, Cicero, Cornelius Nepos, Plutarch, and Lucian, it may be concluded that its aims were closely associated, if not identical with, the intent and purposes of epideictic oratory as described by the rhetoricians. As a genre, it most certainly had at its axis the techniques of amplification and comparison, in addition to those rules of praise codified in the formal encomium. It may be said, therefore, that the genre was concerned with a portrait of the individual, the presentation of the *bios* pattern from birth to death (according to the designs of the author), and that the particular contents of that pattern usually included praiseworthy actions, deeds, accomplishments, sayings, and so forth, either in toto or in part.

3

Genre Examples

> Let us now sing the praises of famous men,
>   the heroes of our nation's history. . . .
> All these won fame in their own generation
>   and were the pride of their times. . . .
> Their prosperity is handed on to their descendants,
>   and their inheritance to future generations. . . .
> Their line will endure for all time,
>   and their fame will never be blotted out.
> Their bodies are buried in peace,
>   but their name lives for ever. (Ecclus. 44:1, 7, 11, 13–14, NEB)

It would now seem profitable, before comparing the gospels with the genre defined in the previous chapter, to examine more fully some of the treatises related to this type of laudatory biography. Examples to be considered have been selected from the works of Isocrates, Xenophon, Philo, Tacitus, Lucian, Josephus, and Philostratus.

Three works by Isocrates clearly belong to this genre—*Helen, Busiris,* and *Evagoras*. The first two, according to Isocrates, were written as correctives to earlier works (*Helen,* a corrective to Gorgias's treatment of Helen, and *Busiris,* a corrective to a work of the same title by an author identified as Polycrates) and, as such, are intended to illustrate how such literary tasks could be performed more appropriately. They are, therefore, intended as literary models and were so considered by other writers after Isocrates. *Evagoras* was a treatise commissioned by Nicocles to be presented at a festival to commemorate his father, Evagoras. It is one of the earliest extant encomia, and illustrates the affinity of the encomium to the funeral oration. In each of these works, the subject is declared to be worthy of the ensuing literary treatment, and in *Evagoras,* Isocrates makes the point that his task was especially difficult, a rhetorical device itself in that the successful accomplishment of the task enhances the stature of the author.

Helen is of particular interest for both the *topoi* and the techniques employed. The starting point for this "model" encomium is Helen's descent (*Helen* 16). She is distinguished by having Zeus as her father: "For although Zeus begat every man of the demigods, of this woman alone he condescended to be called father." While Gorgias's encomium of Helen also includes the praiseworthiness of her parentage, Isocrates omits all references to the glory derived from her mother's side of the family. Chief among Helen's many qualities is her beauty, the source of which is said to have been Zeus. Then, by comparison, Isocrates elevates her to a rank equal with, if not above that of Heracles:

> While he [Zeus] was devoted most of all to the son of Alcmena [Heracles], and to the sons of Leda, yet his preference for Helen, as compared with Heracles, was so great that, although he conferred upon his son strength of body, which is able to overpower all others by force, yet to her he gave the gift of beauty, which by its nature brings even strength itself into subjection to it. (16)

The comparison of Helen with Heracles continues with reference to the source from which each attracted admiration from their admirers: Heracles from wars and combats, a life of danger and hardship, Helen from her nature and a life of ease:

> And knowing that all distinction and renown accrue, not from a life of ease, but from wars and perilous combats, and since he wished, not only to exalt their persons to the gods, but also to bequeath to them glory that would be immortal, he gave his son a life of labours and love of perils, and to Helen he granted the gift of nature which drew the admiration of all beholders and which in all men inspired contention. (17)

Much of Helen's praiseworthiness is derived from the character of her suitors. Following a rather lengthy digression revolving around Theseus (one of her suitors whose significance will be discussed later), Isocrates specifically states that he has used the illustrious reputation of Theseus as a basis for the worthiness of Helen's character:

> As for Helen, daughter of Zeus, who established her power over such excellence and sobriety, should she not be praised and honoured, and regarded as far superior to all the women who have ever lived? For surely we shall never have a more trustworthy witness or more competent judge of Helen's good attributes than the opinion of Theseus. (38)

He then continues to show how the conflict over Helen, which eventually led to the Trojan War, was inevitable because of both the num-
bers of those who sought her favor (39–40) and Alexander's choice of
Helen above all others (41–45). In the latter case, heritage is again a
factor: Alexander "could leave no more glorious heritage to his children than by seeing to it that they should be descendants of Zeus, not
only on their father's side, but also on their mother's" (44, a statement
which is of further interest in view of Isocrates' own omission of
Helen's maternal ancestry). Isocrates continues to explain Alexander's
choice:

> For he knew that while other blessings bestowed by Fortune soon change
> hands, nobility of birth abides forever with the same possessors; there-
> fore he foresaw that this choice would be to the advantage of all his race,
> whereas the other gifts would be enjoyed for the duration of his own life
> only. (44)

Praise can be heaped upon Helen, even from the ensuing tragic
war. It is drawn from the willingness of both the Greeks and the
Trojans to fight for the honor of claiming her residency:

> And they were not acting in this way as eager champions of Alexander or
> of Menelaus; nay, the Trojans were upholding the cause of Asia, the
> Greeks of Europe, in the belief that the land in which Helen in person
> resided would be the more favoured of Fortune. (51)

So intense was this belief that even the gods did not dissuade their
own children from battle, even though they could foresee their off-
springs' fate (52).

Isocrates then turned his attention to the primary reason for praising Helen, her beauty. Here amplification is the operative principle:
it was of the "highest degree," of all things "the most venerated," "the
most precious," and "the most divine." Refusing to stop with Gorgias's
recognition that she possessed extraordinary beauty, Isocrates goes on
to relate beauty to the other virtues:

> And it is easy to determine its power; for while many things which do
> not have any attributes of courage, wisdom, or justice will be seen to be
> more highly valued than any one of these attributes, yet of those things
> which lack beauty we shall find not one that is beloved; on the contrary,
> all are despised except in so far as they possess in some degree this
> outward form, beauty, and it is for this reason that virtue is most highly
> esteemed, because it is the most beautiful of ways of living. (54)

He concludes by relating beauty to divinity: "The greatest proof of my statement is this: we shall find that more mortals have been made immortal because of their beauty than for all other excellences" (60). Of course, the implication is that Helen had attained a divine state.

The last portion relates some of her activities which reveal her power and her divine status in relation to men. Helen was granted the power to raise mortals to divine stations. First, she raised her brothers in this way, and thereafter they were able to save sailors in peril when called upon to do so (61). She also saved and raised Menelaus to divine status (62). Then Isocrates inserts the story of the restoration of sight to Stesichorus:

> And she displayed her own power to the poet Stesichorus also; for when, at the beginning of his ode, he spoke in disparagement of her, he arose deprived of his sight; but when he recognized the cause of his misfortune and composed the *Recantation,* as it is called, she restored to him his normal sight. (64)

He relates an appearance story in which Helen appeared to Homer, commanding him "to compose a poem on those who went on the expedition to Troy," in honor of their death. Isocrates adds that the relationship of Helen to mankind is to be seen in her power to punish:

> Since, then, Helen has power to punish as well as to reward, it is the duty of those who have great wealth to propitiate and to honour her with thank-offerings, sacrifices, and processions, and philosophers should endeavour to speak of her in a manner worthy of her merits; for such are the first-fruits it is fitting that men of cultivation should offer. (66)

Thus, in her divine state, Helen has the power to elevate to divine status, to punish, and to reward—ample reason to make her the object of one's supplications (perhaps a "cultic" motive behind *Helen* 66?).

Isocrates concludes his "model" encomium by relating what he sees to be Helen's major accomplishment: "it is owing to Helen that we are not the slaves of the barbarians." He continues:

> For we shall find that it was because of her that the Greeks became united in harmonious accord and organized a common expedition against the barbarians and that it was then for the first time that Europe set up a trophy of victory over Asia. . . . (67)

This survey reveals sufficient grounds for classifying *Helen* as epideictic oratory. It contains both amplification and comparison, and it uses the *topoi* of the encomium as deemed appropriate. Only a few of the *topoi* prescribed by the rhetoricians have actually been employed by Isocrates; that is, only those needed for his purpose. The use of the technique of comparison is especially instructive and deserves additional attention.

The use of comparison in portraying Helen's suitors has been noted, but the attention given in the treatise to Theseus is extraordinary. This digression could be considered a forerunner of the format adopted by both Cornelius Nepos and Plutarch. In his discussion of Helen's suitors, Isocrates has chosen to emphasize the illustrious character of only one, Theseus. This treatment is unusual because he actually suspends the subject of Helen. It is striking that Isocrates' discussion of Theseus occupies over one-third of the entire encomium of Helen, which he is offering as a "model." Throughout the Theseus section proper, Helen's name rarely occurs, and there is only one reference to the fact that Helen, not Theseus, is the original subject. Form critically, one could argue (rather convincingly I think) that Isocrates has cleverly inserted a separate treatise, originally intended to praise Theseus, into the narrative on Helen. The oddity and length of the digression, plus the internal unity of the Theseus section, argue for the probability of its being a separate work incorporated into the narrative on Helen. Furthermore, section 39 and following may be moved to a position immediately after section 17 (thereby omitting the section on Theseus and transitional statements) without seriously impairing the unity of the encomium of Helen. The model encomium, as measured by the prescriptions of the rhetoricians, is, in fact, the section on Theseus.[1]

The transitional statement developed by Isocrates to introduce the Theseus section reveals that he is, indeed, aware of the problems created by his literary procedure. He responds specifically to ease the situation he himself has created by focusing solely upon Theseus. First, he acknowledges immediately the relationship of Theseus to Helen: Theseus is one of Helen's admirers, and her abduction by him may be attributed to his love for her. It is his admirable character and superior accomplishments which cause this work to be considered "an encomium of Helen" and not "an accusation of Theseus" (21). Second, in the midst of the Theseus section (29), Isocrates admits "But . . . I perceive that I am being carried beyond the proper limits of my theme and I fear that some may think that I am more concerned with Theseus than with the subject [here unspecified] which I originally chose." Third, after summarizing the major contributions of Theseus, Isocrates explains his digression in a short transitional paragraph:

> As for Helen [the first time she is mentioned by name since *Helen* 17, with the single exception of 21, which is more of an editorial comment than a reference integral to the narrative], daughter of Zeus, who established her power over such excellence and sobriety, should she not be praised and honoured, and regarded as far superior to all the women who have ever lived? For surely we shall never have a more trustworthy witness or more competent judge of Helen's good attributes than the opinion of Theseus. But lest I seem through poverty of ideas to be dwelling unduly upon the same theme and by misusing the glory of one man to be praising Helen, I wish now to review the subsequent events also. (38)

Turning now to the portrait of Theseus, one notices that Isocrates begins (as with Helen) with references to his family background: "reputedly the son of Aegeus, but in reality the progeny of Poseidon" (18). A statement of Theseus's desire for and abduction of Helen follows. He points out that Helen's abduction was not the act of any ordinary person, an observation which leads him into an assessment of Theseus's superior qualities.

> If the achiever of these exploits had been an ordinary person and not one of the very distinguished, it would not yet be clear whether this discourse is an encomium of Helen or an accusation of Theseus; but as it is, while in the case of other men who have won renown we shall find that one deficient in courage, another in wisdom, and another in some kindred virtue, yet this hero alone was lacking in naught, but had attained consummate virtue. (21)

Helen is to draw glory from being "loved and admired" by such a person. At this point, Isocrates devotes his attention entirely to the portrait of Theseus.

Heracles becomes important again for comparison. "The fairest praise that I can award Theseus is this—that he, a contemporary of Heracles, won a fame which rivalled his" (23). The comparison leads to the following proposition, which Isocrates then proves by example: "It came to pass that Heracles undertook perilous labours more celebrated and more severe, Theseus those more useful and, to the Greeks, of more viral importance" (23ff.).

Isocrates summarizes his portrait of Theseus in sections 31 through 37, with a list of his virtues and his accomplishments while serving as governor of the city. Consequently,

> . . . Theseus passed his life beloved of his people and not the object of their plots, not preserving his sovereignty by means of alien military force, but protected, as by a bodyguard, by the goodwill of the citizens, by virtue of his authority ruling as a king, but by his benefactions as a popular leader; for so equitably and so well did he administer the city that even to this day traces of his clemency may be seen remaining. (37)

At this point, Isocrates returns to his original topic, Helen, his digression on Theseus having made the praiseworthy nature of Helen even more convincing.

The second work by Isocrates to be examined here is *Busiris*. Busiris apparently was a mythical king of Egypt. Isocrates had obviously read Polybius's earlier eulogy and felt compelled to compose a corrective on the following grounds:

> For although everyone knows that those who wish to praise a person must attribute to him a larger number of good qualities than he really possesses, and accusers must do the contrary, you have so far fallen short of following these principles of rhetoric that, though you profess to defend Busiris, you have not only failed to absolve him of the calumny with which he is attacked, but have even imputed to him a lawlessness of such enormity that it is impossible for one to invent wickedness more atrocious. (*Busiris* 5)

Busiris, like *Helen*, belongs to the epideictic group of oratory, but Isocrates does not refer to it as an encomium. He considers it an "apology" (*apologia*, 4 and 9). He considered Gorgias's *Helen* an apology, but the principles of portraiture employed by Isocrates are not essentially different from those utilized by Gorgias. One concludes that the line separating the two "forms" is, indeed, a fine one.

Isocrates begins his portrait of Busiris by referring to his noble lineage:

> Of the noble lineage of Busiris who would not find it easy to speak? His father was Poseidon, his mother Libya the daughter of Epephus the son of Zeus, and she, they say, was the first woman to rule as queen and to give her own name to her country. (10)

Next, he refers to the accomplishments of Busiris. Busiris expanded his mother's domain, conquering "many peoples" and acquiring "supreme power." He "established his royal seat in Egypt." His choice of this country is so commendable as to warrant a brief section in praise of Egypt (12–14). Then Isocrates lists Busiris's administrative accomplishments (15–29), including, at the top of the list, his "reverence for the gods." Although one has no idea what were the criticisms of Busiris to which Polycrates addressed himself, it may be surmised that the defense portion of Isocrates' work is contained in this longer section which consists of the political and administrative accomplishments of the hero. For all practical purposes, Isocrates has concluded his portrait of Busiris, because following the long section on the accomplishments, he returns to his polemic against Polycrates.

The third work from the hand of Isocrates is his *Evagoras*. Isocrates begins this encomium (*dia logōn egkōmiaxein, Evagoras* 8) by relating the purpose of his present efforts: "But the spoken word which should adequately recount the deeds of Evagoras would make his virtues never to be forgotten among all mankind" (4). Following a rather lengthy discussion of the difficulty of the subject, which accentuates the superiority of the author who has undertaken such a task, Isocrates proceeds with the "birth and ancestry of Evagoras" (12). He recounts not only the list of ancestors but also their glories, so that he can show how Evagoras "proved himself not inferior to the noblest and greatest examples of excellence which were of his inheritance." Also in this section, Isocrates refers to the history of Salamis before Evagoras's birth. Two key sentences describe the beginning of Evagoras's life: "So distinguished from the beginning was the heritage transmitted to Evagoras by his ancestors" (19) and "Such was the state of affairs in Salamis, and the descendants of the usurper were in possession of the throne when Evagoras was born" (21). Thus the accounts of lineage and historical setting have prepared the way for the advent of Evagoras into the world.

Isocrates' treatment of Evagoras's birth is very interesting. He alludes to but does not give details of miraculous events:

> I prefer to say nothing of the portents, the oracles, the visions appearing in dreams, from which the impression might be gained that he was of superhuman birth, not because I disbelieve the reports, but that I may make it clear to all that I am so far from resorting to invention in

speaking of his deeds that even of those matters which are in fact true I
dismiss such as are known only to the few and of which not all the
citizens are cognizant. (21)

Despite the disclaimer, the reader is obviously meant to conclude
that such events did occur at Evagoras' birth.

Isocrates continues his portrait by referring to some of Evagoras's
characteristics, some of which, it will be noted, correspond with those
connected with encomia, as described by the rhetoricians. "When
Evagoras was a boy he possessed beauty, bodily strength, and modesty, the very qualities that are most becoming to that age" (22).
When Evagoras reached manhood, he not only retained the above
qualities but added manly courage, wisdom, and justness, each "in
extraordinary degree." The kings' response to the arrival of such a
person upon the political scene is vividly described:

> So surpassing was his excellence of both body and mind that when the
> kings of that time looked upon him they were terrified and feared for
> their throne, thinking that a man of such nature could not possibly pass
> this life in the status of a private citizen, but whenever they observed his
> character, they felt such confidence in him that they believed that even
> if anyone else should dare to injure them, Evagoras would be their
> champion. (24)

Isocrates then tells of one political aspirant who tried to have Evagoras
killed after he (the aspirant) had assassinated the tyrant ruler. The attempt was made because he thought Evagoras was the only obstacle
between him and the throne. Evagoras was only able to save himself
by fleeing to Cilicia (25–27). His spirit was not humbled in exile as
had been the case with so many others under similar circumstances
(comparison). Rather, Evagoras determined to acquire the throne and,
upon his return, attacked the palace with only fifty men. It was "as if
a god were their leader, they one and all held fast to their promises,
and Evagoras, just as if either he had an army superior to that of his
adversaries or foresaw the outcome, held to his resolution" [i.e., his
guiding principle: "to act only in self-defence and never to be the
aggressor"]. (28–32)

The valor (*aretē*) he demonstrated in his rise to power and the
greatness of his deeds having been thus related (33), Isocrates proceeds to show that no sovereign since the beginning of time had won

his "honour more gloriously than Evagoras." This long section contains comparison between Evagoras and Cyrus and Conon, including analyses of military qualities, of the governed, and of their respective accomplishments. Neither man excels Evagoras; rather Evagoras gloriously excels each one of them.

Isocrates concludes by trying to evaluate the person about whom he has written. The key word is *immortal*: "if any men of the past have by their merit become immortal, Evagoras also has earned this preferment. . . ." At another point, he refers sweepingly to the poets in a similar context:

> In view of these facts, if any of the poets have used extravagant expressions in characterizing any man of the past, asserting that he was a god among men, or a mortal divinity, all praise of that kind would be especially in harmony with the noble qualities of Evagoras. (72)

Isocrates then admonishes Nicocles to emulate Evagoras and to pursue the study of philosophy, which reveals the didactic function of the present encomium. It also lends support to Birger Gerhardsson's thesis concerning the narration of the fathers, especially among the Hellenistic traditions:

> In Antiquity what was narrated concerning the fathers had a practical purpose: that of providing examples to be emulated, warnings, or other definite lessons. Jewish, Hellenistic and Christian traditions in the sources are all *tendentious*, whether edifying or otherwise didactic.[2]

There is no reference to Evagoras's death, and it is extremely difficult to know what is intended by this omission. Aristotle referred to Evagoras's death as murder,[3] which would not be a proper ending to so illustrious a portrait as that drawn by Isocrates. Isocrates did not feel the need to present any account of Evagoras's death, and the omission was his prerogative as an encomiast.

The *Agesilaus* of Xenophon was modeled after Isocrates' *Evagoras*, though Xenophon "was not the man to follow Isocrates blindly."[4] D. R. Stuart writes of its literary style: "the structural plan of the *Agesilaus* shows a compartment-like exactness characteristic of the rhetorical patterns emanating from Gorgias and his kind."[5] Its place is, therefore, within the classification of epideictic oratory—concerned with both praise and vindication. It is the organization of the treatise that is of interest for this study rather than the way the subject is praised, since this resembles that of the previous examples.

Xenophon begins his treatise in a typically formal manner:

> I know how difficult it is to write an appreciation of Agesilaus that shall be worthy of his virtue and glory. Nevertheless the attempt must be made. For it would not be seemly that so good a man, just because of his perfection, should receive no tributes of praise, however inadequate. (*Agesilaus* I. 1; see also *Ad Herennium* III. 6. 11–12)

Then, after references to Agesilaus's praiseworthy descent, which he traces back to Heracles, and a brief discussion of his nurture and early childhood, Xenophon moves to the stature of the country over which he was to rule so long and so gloriously, a country worthy of him. The early signs of Agesilaus's excellence (*aretē*) are mentioned only in that he was chosen at a very early age to assume leadership (I. 5–8).

For the most part, the account of his reign is in chronological order, interrupted occasionally by references to the king's character, which is revealed by his deeds (see I. 20, 27, 36; II. 8, 12, 21, and so on). This section on his rule is the first of Xenophon's illustrations of his hero's greatness.

Chapter 3 begins another section in which Xenophon specifically treats the virtues of Agesilaus. In the first paragraph, he outlines the intended plan of the entire work:

> Such, then, is the record of my hero's deeds, so far as they were done before a crowd of witnesses. Actions like these need no proofs; the mere mention of them is enough and they command belief immediately. But now I will attempt to show the virtue that was in his soul, the virtue through which he wrought those deeds and loved all that is honourable and put away all that is base. (II. 1; see also Quintilian, *Inst*. III. 7. 10–18, on pp. 122–23).

The virtues to be developed (piety, justice, self-control, courage, and wisdom) are standard, as is the order in which they are discussed.[6] This section contains statements attributed to Agesilaus which illustrate each of his virtues under discussion. It also contains comparisons of Agesilaus with "the Persian king" (VII. 6; IX. 1–2), to demonstrate his superiority over the latter. Emulation is also encouraged in this section:

> If line and rule are a noble discovery of man as aids to the production of good work, I think that the virtue of Agesilaus may well stand as a noble

example for those to follow who wish to make moral goodness a habit. For who that imitates a pious, a just, a sober, a self-controlled man, can come to be unrighteousness, unjust, violent, wanton? (X. 2)

Xenophon concludes the treatise with a summary of the virtues discussed, with only a brief reference to Agesilaus's death:

> So complete was the record of his service to his fatherland that it did not end even when he died: he was still a bountiful benefactor of the state when he was brought home to be laid in his eternal resting-place, and, having raised up monuments of his virtue throughout the world, was buried with royal ceremony in his own land. (XI. 16)

The importance of Xenophon's *Agesilaus* for the present study is threefold: first, it represents the standard pattern by which to praise the individual within the category of epideictic oratory; second, the structure was based upon both chronological and thematic principles as seen in both the rules of Quintilian and the works of Suetonius, especially his *Deified Julius*; and, third, Xenophon organizes both sayings and deeds in a manner unique in the literature from that period currently available for investigation.

The next example, Philo, is taken from some four centuries later, partly because of the scarcity of sources from the intervening period and partly because he is more nearly contemporary with the gospels. The point of this section, however, is not to trace the historical development of the encomium (or epideictic oratory in general) but to illustrate how the lives of the famous were portrayed.

Philo's *De vita Mosis*[7] was cited by Hadas and Smith to represent the aretalogical tradition. If one is convinced by Hadas and Smith's discussion, then one should note what must have been the close relationship between aretalogy and epideictic literature. F. H. Colson, for example, comments on the lives written by Philo (Abraham, Joseph, and Moses):

> . . . the separate stories are admirably told with much fire, vigour and lucidity. The "stilted and frigid" speeches repel us, but to Greek readers living in the age of Epideictic oratory, they would be congenial enough.[8]

According to E. R. Goodenough, Philo is concerned with describing Moses "in terms of the king–saviour conception of his day: he is the perfect king, lawmaker, priest, and prophet."[9] Moses clearly represents the "pattern of the ideal man and savior." In his idealistic pre-

sentation of Moses, Philo's allegorical methodology is less conspic-
uous than in his other works.[10] In addition, he employs amplification
freely,[11] as, for example, in his account of Moses' education (*De vita
Mosis* I. 21ff.), which conforms to one's expectations of an Egyptian
prince, in spite of the absence of evidence from the biblical narratives. Comparison is also used, and it may be concluded that this life
of Moses belongs to the same general category as the other works
offered for consideration. D. L. Tiede refers to *De vita Mosis* as a
"complete encomium."[12] It is this, perhaps, which accounts for the
peculiarities cited by Colson:

> Philo's arrangement of the life of Moses under the four heads of king,
> lawgiver, priest and prophet does, no doubt, serve for a logical basis to
> the work, but it leads him into many oddities. While the story of Moses
> as king or leader is carried on consistently to the end of Exodus xviii.,
> what next to the deliverance itself is the central point of the story, the
> theophany on Sinai, is entirely omitted; the account of Balaam and Balak,
> which has little to do with Moses himself, is given a disproportionate
> length, while the stories of the Red Sea and the Manna and the Golden
> Calf are given twice over.[13]

These peculiarities may be attributed to the author's use of sources
for specific aims, in accordance with established literary principles
evident in epideictic oratory.

Philo states his purpose at the beginning of the treatise and reiter-
ates it at the conclusion—to call to the reader's attention the story of
the greatest and most perfect of men:

> I purpose to write the life of Moses, whom some describe as the legis-
> lator of the Jews, others as the interpreter of the Holy Laws. I hope to
> bring the story of this greatest and most perfect of men to the knowledge
> of such as deserve not to remain in ignorance of it; for, while the fame of
> the laws which he left behind him has travelled throughout the civilized
> world and reached the ends of the earth, the man himself as he really
> was is known to few. Greek men of letters have refused to treat him as
> worthy of memory, possibly through envy, and also because in many
> cases the ordinances of the legislators of the different states are opposed
> to his. . . . But I will disregard their malice, and tell the story of Moses
> as I have learned it, both from the sacred books, the wonderful monu-
> ments of his wisdom which he has left behind him, and from some of the
> elders of the nation; for I always interwove what I was told with what I
> read, and thus believed myself to have a closer knowledge than others of
> his life's history. (I. 1–2, 4)

> Such, as recorded in the Holy Scriptures, was the life and such the end of Moses, king, lawgiver, high priest, prophet. (II. 292)

The presentation under the four categories (king, lawgiver, high priest, and prophet) is the organizational structure of the treatise and is certainly consistent with accepted principles of writing an encomium (see, for example, Xenophon's *Agesilaus* III. 1 and Quintilian, *Inst.* III. 7. 10–18)[14] and is further affirmed by Philo in the transition statements between books I and II of *De vita Mosis*:

> We have now told the story of Moses' actions in his capacity of king. We must next deal with all that he achieved by his powers as high priest and legislator, powers which he possessed as the most fitting accomplishments of kingship. (I. 334; see also II. 1–6)

The contents of book I are summarized at the beginning of book II, emphasizing that what has been described (presented largely in a chronological order) is praiseworthy.

> The former treatise dealt with the birth and nurture of Moses; also with his education and career as a ruler, in which capacity his conduct was not merely blameless but highly praiseworthy; also with the works which he performed in Egypt and during the journeys both at the Red Sea and in the wilderness—works which no words can adequately describe; further, with the troubles which he successfully surmounted, and with his partial distribution of territories to the combatants. (II. 1)

Following such introductory remarks (II. 1–6), the material is organized thematically to support the thesis that Moses was not only a king but also a lawgiver, high priest, and prophet. There is notable similarity between this work and Xenophon's *Agesilaus*.

The portrait of Moses begins with his birth and ancestry. "I will begin with what is necessarily the right place to begin. Moses was by race a Chaldean but was born and reared in Egypt" (I. 5). "He had for his father and mother the best of their contemporaries, members of the same tribe, though with them mutual affection was a stronger tie than family connections. He was seventh in descent from the first settler who became the founder of the whole Jewish nation [Abraham]" (I. 7). Then Philo interprets the biblical account of Moses' birth and recounts his early childhood and educational excellences. Such phrases as "his beauty and fine condition" (I. 15), "noble and goodly to look upon" (I. 18), "he applied himself to hearing and seeing what was sure to profit the soul" (I. 20), and "his gifted nature forestalled

their instruction" punctuate this portion of the narrative in a manner
designed to call forth the reader's admiration. Moses' accomplishments and qualities were such that his associates could hardly discern
whether his true nature was human or divine or some mixture of the
two (I. 27). Indeed, here was a man of true and rare greatness:

> And, in his desire to live to the soul alone and not to the body, he made
> a special practice of frugal contentment, and had an unparalleled scorn
> for a life of luxury. He exemplified his philosophical creed by his daily
> actions. His words expressed his feelings, and his actions accorded with
> his words, so that speech and life were in harmony, and thus through
> their mutual agreement were found to make melody together as on a
> musical instrument. (I. 29)

His first flight from Egypt is attributed to the envy and fear of the
king's intimates, who proceeded to convince him that his rule was
threatened by Moses (I. 46). Even during the exile, the strength of
his character is demonstrated by his continued development and discipline carried out under the guidance of "an admirable trainer, the
reason within him" (I. 48). His experience as a shepherd, at which
Moses proved more skillful than any other (I. 63), provided unex-
pected training for the command he later assumed (I. 60ff.). His response to God's commissioning him is cited to show his modesty (I.
84).

The relationship of Moses to God illustrates the *biographical* function of the narrative, which revolves around the person of Moses. To
be sure, he is an instrument of God's activity, but he is the central
figure nevertheless. For example, I. 148 and following is a summary
of Moses' function.

> The appointed leader of all these was Moses, invested with this office
> and kingship, not like some of those who thrust themselves into positions
> of power by means of arms and engines of war and strength of infantry,
> cavalry and navy, but on account of his goodness and his nobility of
> conduct and the universal benevolence which he never failed to show.
> Further, his office was bestowed upon him by God, the lover of virtue
> and nobility, as the reward due to him. For, when he gave up the
> lordship of Egypt, which he held as son to the then reigning king,
> because the sight of the iniquities committed in the land and his own
> nobility of soul and magnanimity of spirit and inborn hatred of evil led
> him to renounce completely his expected inheritance from the kinsfolk
> of his adoption, He Who presides over and takes charge of all things
> thought good to requite him with the kingship of a nation more populous

and mightier, a nation destined to be consecrated above all others to offer prayers forever on behalf of the human race that it may be delivered from evil and participate in what is good. (I. 148–49; *see also* I 198)

More specifically, this relationship is described as a partnership with God:

And so, as he abjured the accumulation of lucre, and the wealth whose influence is mighty among men, God rewarded him by giving him instead the greatest and most perfect wealth. That is the wealth of the whole earth and sea and rivers, and of all the other elements and the combination which they form. For, since God judged him worthy to appear as a partner of His own possessions, He gave into his hands the whole world as a portion well fitted for His heir. Therefore, each element obeyed him as its master, changed its natural properties and submitted to his command, and this perhaps is no wonder. (I. 155–56)

Thus Moses stands out not only as illustrious, but also as a savior model:

Thus he beheld what is hidden from the sight of mortal nature, and, in himself and his life displayed for all to see, he has set before us, like some well-wrought picture, a piece of work beautiful and godlike, a model for those who are willing to copy it. Happy are they who imprint, or strive to imprint, that image in their souls. (I. 158–59)[15]

It is not possible to deal exhaustively with the whole of Philo's treatise on Moses, but one should note his use of comparison. Perhaps the clearest example occurs in the second book, in his discussion of Moses as lawgiver. It begins with a general statement:

That Moses himself was the best of all lawgivers in all countries, better in fact than any that have ever arisen among either the Greeks or the barbarians, and that his laws are most excellent and truly come from God, since they omit nothing that is needful, is shewn most clearly. . . . (II. 12)

Later, the laws attributed to or delivered through Moses are compared with those of other nations.

The Athenians rejected the customs and institutions of the Lacedaemonians, and the Lacedaemonians those of the Athenians. . . . We may fairly say that mankind from east to west, every country and nation and state, shew aversion to foreign institutions, and think that they will enhance the respect for their own by shewing disrespect for those of other countries. It is not so with ours. They attract and win the attention of all, of

barbarians, of Greeks, of dwellers on the mainland and islands, of nations of the east and the west, of Europe and Asia, of the whole inhab-
ited world from end to end. (II. 19–20)

The above statement calls to mind the praise of Helen to be derived
from the stature of her suitors. Still later, Ptolemy is cited as another
proof of Moses' superiority:

Ptolemy, surnamed Philadelphus, was the third in succession to Alexander, the conqueror of Egypt. In all the qualities which make a good
ruler, he excelled not only his contemporaries, but all who have arisen in
the past; and even till to-day, after so many generations, his praises are
sung for the many evidences and monuments of his greatness of mind
which he left behind him in different cities and countries, so that even
now, acts of more than ordinary munificence of buildings on a specially
great scale are proverbially called Philadelphia after him. To put it
shortly, as the house of the Ptolemies was highly distinguished, compared with other dynasties, so was Philadelphus among the Ptolemies.
(II. 29–30)

It is precisely this man Ptolemy whose qualities are incontestable and
unequalled in the past or present (even by Moses?) who recognized
the innate value of Moses' law and commissioned the translation of
the Septuagint (II. 31ff.), which was miraculously completed through
the dictates of God. (II. 37)

As with most treatises of this type, Philo refers in his conclusion to
Moses' death, the occasion of his supreme glorification (II. 288ff.), the
details of which were revealed to Moses before its occurrence. Also,
as at the death of all who possess true greatness, "all the nations wept
and mourned for him". (II. 291)

The purposes behind Tacitus's *Agricola* have been the subject of
considerable debate.[16] Tacitus was Agricola's son-in-law, and in tone
the treatise closely resembles a funeral oration. Its length, however,
argues against this interpretation. It is quite similar in other respects
to an apology, and comes close to stating an apologetic intent in the
last part of section 3. Its portraiture, like that noted previously in
Isocrates' *Evagoras* and Xenophon's *Agesilaus*, brings it close to the
panegyric (encomium), even though the abundance of material related to Britain suggests at least a pretense to history. These problems, however, do not jeopardize its placement in the category of
epideictic oratory. Whereas Tacitus's competence in "physical science," "geography," and "military science" has been questioned by

some, his rhetorical skill and biographical intent are unassailable.[17]
Generally speaking, therefore, we are in agreement with the assessment of R. M. Ogilvie and Ian Richmond:

> The *Agricola* is a biography. Its full title is *de vita Iulii Agricolae,* and Tacitus makes it plain that he has set out to write a life of his father-in-law in the accustomed manner (c. I. 4 *narraturo mihi vitam defuncti hominis*; c. 46. 4 *Agricola posteritati narratus*)—*narrare vitam* is the phrase which Nepos used to distinguish the character of his Lives from other historical works . . . the *Agricola* remains first and foremost an account of Agricola's life and achievements. . . . There is, therefore, a tendency in the *Agricola,* as in his other writings, for events to be accommodated to the characters as Tacitus saw them, and this tendency is liable to entail distortion. But Tacitus knew and loved Agricola and the biography which he has left us is an intimate and penetrating record of a man.[18]

In the beginning, the treatise refers to the practice of writing about famous men:

> To hand down to posterity the works and ways of famous men was our fathers' custom: our age has not yet abandoned it even now, indifferent though it be to its own children, whenever, at least, some great and notable virtue has dominated and overpowered the vice common alike to small states and great—misapprehension of integrity and jealousy.
> But in our fathers' times, just as the doing of deeds worth recording was natural and more obvious, so also there was inducement then to the brightest spirits to publish such records of virtue. (*Agricola* 1)

This reference calls to mind the statements of Isocrates and Xenophon about the benefits of imitating such famous personages. Indeed, at the end of the speech (46), imitation is proposed specifically as the natural response to the character of Agricola:

> Let reverence rather, let unending thankfulness, let imitation even, if our strength permit, be our tribute to your memory: this is true respect, this is kinship's duty. This would I say to wife and daughter, so to venerate the memory of husband and of father as to ponder each word and deed within their hearts, and to cleave to the lineaments and features of the soul rather than of the body.

The portrait itself begins in section 4 with a reference to Agricola's family: "Gnaeus Julius Agricola was a scion of the ancient and illustrious Roman colony of Forum Julii. . . ." Each of his grandfathers was "Procurator of Caesar," an office which Tacitus defines in terms

which confer greatness on the occupant. His father attained the rank
of senator and excelled in both rhetoric and philosophy. "His mother
was Julia Procilla, a woman of rare virtue. From her fond bosom he
imbibed his education. . . ." His early training is described in some
detail, and "he achieved the rarest of feats; he was a student, yet
preserved his balance." He spent an illustrious apprenticeship in Britain, where he gained insight into the conditions of the province and
cultivated the virtue of humility (5). He married Domitia Decidiana,
"a woman of high lineage," a marriage which itself provides ample
reason to praise him (6).

Next follows a series of events which depict both Agricola's development as a leader and some of the qualities that mark his greatness.

> Agricola accordingly restrained his own energy and applied a check to
> his enthusiasm, in order that it might not grow too strong; he was
> trained to habits of deference, and skilful in tempering duty with expe-
> diency. . . . He traced his success to the responsible general whose agent
> he was: so by scrupulous obedience and modesty in self-advertisement
> he escaped envy without missing distinction. (5)

And, later:

> Agricola, thanks to his native shrewdness, though surrounded with civil-
> ians, administered without friction, yet without sacrifice of justice. . . .
> When the decisions of the council chamber demanded he was serious,
> keen, strict, yet generally merciful; when he had fulfilled the demands of
> office he dropped the official mask: reserve, pompousness, and greed he
> put away from him; and yet in his case, the rarest of cases, neither did
> amiability impair authority nor strictness affection. It would be an insult
> to the qualities of a man so great to dwell here upon his probity and
> self-control. Fame itself, which even good men often court, he never
> sought by parading his virtues or by artifice; incapable of rivalry among
> his colleagues, incapable of wrangling with the Imperial Agents, he
> counted it inglorious to succeed in such fields, and contemptible to let
> himself feel sore. (9)

The next portion of *Agricola* describes Britain and the character
and condition of its peoples and lists those who had ruled Britain
under Roman authority (10–17). This sets the stage ("Such was the
condition of Britain" [18]) and specifies the tasks confronting Agricola
when he assumed command ("such the alternations of war and peace
which Agricola found . . ." [18]). Then follows a chronological account
of his successful rule (18–39), punctuated with tributes to his excel-

lences. There are two direct statements that he was the "first" to do something (20, 25) and the climactic account of his defeat of Calgacus, leader of the opposing coalition of tribes. The conflict with Calgacus is portrayed as greatness in opposition to greatness, which thereby illustrates the significance of Agricola's superiority. This is especially evident in the comparison of both their speeches immediately before the final battle. These reflect the native abilities of each general and vividly portray the respective enthusiasm to do battle generated among those who heard each of them. Even so, it is apparent that Agricola's is the better, for his speech was often interrupted enthusiastically (33). Though outnumbered, Agricola placed himself at the front of the battle line (35), and his resulting victory was second to none.

Tacitus is quick to point out that Agricola was not in search of glory for himself. At a time when Rome was hungry for triumphs, it was this course of action that precluded the envy and suspicion of his superiors (39–41).[19] He handed to his successor a peaceful province and returned to an unassuming welcome home. While Rome suffered setbacks elsewhere, Agricola brought victory with him, and he avoided self-destruction by remaining in the background. In this way, he lived to a ripe old age, spared of the grief which would have been his had he been aware of subsequent events (44), and his death was mourned by all (43ff.). "Happy your fate, Agricola! happy not only in the lustre of your life, but in a timely death" (45). The conclusion is consistent with the whole speech:

> Whatever we have loved in Agricola, whatever we have admired, abides, and will abide, in the hearts of men, in the procession of the ages, in the records of history. Many of the Ancients has Forgetfulness engulfed as though neither fame nor name were theirs. Agricola, whose story here is told, will outlive death, to be our children's heritage. (46)

It will be remembered that Lucian was cited earlier for his treatise against encomia that were passed off as histories.[20] His intense invective, however, should not be interpreted as a lack of appreciation for this literary form, if it were employed in the proper setting. A monument to his appreciation of the encomium is the treatise to which we now turn, Lucian's *Life of Demonax*. It is difficult to know the exact occasion for the speech, but in character and structure it is most certainly epideictic, and can be classified even more specifically in the encomium category. It is interesting to note that at least one scholar feels that of all the possible classical parallels to gospel literature, the present treatise is the closest (though it leaves much to be desired).[21] Lucian opens with a statement of his purpose for writing—in a way similar to others previously encountered.

> It was on the cards, it seems, that our modern world should not be altogether destitute of noteworthy and memorable men, but should produce enormous physical prowess and a highly philosophic mind. I speak with reference to the Boeotian Sostratus, whom the Greeks called Heracles and believed to be that hero, and especially to Demonax, the philosopher. . . . It is now fitting to tell of Demonax for two reasons—that he may be retained in memory by men of culture as far as I can bring it about, and that young men of good instincts who aspire to philosophy may not have to shape themselves by ancient precedents alone, but may be able to set themselves a pattern from our modern world and to copy that man, the best of all the philosophers whom I know about. (*Demonax* 1–2)

Lucian is preserving the memory of a noteworthy man who could serve as a model for those who desire to follow him. The passage draws additional force from its reference to Heracles (comparison), which gives both heroes an equal status, albeit for different achievements. The preface is followed immediately by a reference to Demonax's lineage ("a Cypriote by birth"), the significant advantages of which were minimized commendably by Demonax's aspirations to a higher life, philosophy. Accordingly, "he despised all that men count good, and, committing himself unreservedly to liberty and free-speech, was steadfast in leading a straight, sane, irreproachable life and in setting an example to all who saw and heard him by his good judgment and the honesty of his philosophy" (3). The decision to take "his departure from life, leaving behind him a great reputation among Greeks of culture" (4), was not one he arrived at hastily. He was aware of the alternatives, for he had been brought up on the poets and had "trained his body and hardened it for endurance," and had been an accomplished speaker. Next, Lucian describes briefly the philosophical style of Demonax, stating that he had most in common with Socrates and Diogenes, which leads him to describe Demonax's character:

> He never was known to make an uproar or excite himself or get angry, even if he had to rebuke someone; though he assailed sins, he forgave sinners, thinking that one should pattern oneself after doctors, who heal sicknesses but feel no anger at the sick. He considered that it is human to err, divine or all but divine to set right what has gone amiss. (7)

And Lucian continues to amplify:

> For this reason he was everyone's friend, and there was no human being
> whom he did not include in his affections, though he liked the society of
> some better than that of others. . . . And in all this, his every word and
> deed was smiled on by the Graces and by Aphrodite, even; so that, to
> quote the comedian, "persuasion perched upon his lips." (10)

Even a person of such qualities and recognized abilities was not
unopposed, and this prompts a comparison with Socrates.

> He too had his Anytus and his Meletus who combined against him and
> brought the same charges that their predecessors brought against Soc-
> rates, asserting that he had never been known to sacrifice and was the
> only man in the community uninitiated in the Eleusinian mysteries. (11)

Unlike Socrates, however, Demonax succeeded in convincing his opponents of his "love for humanity": "So the Athenians, who already
had stones in both hands to throw at him, became good-natured and
friendly toward him at once, and from that day on they honoured,
respected and finally admired him" (11). This does not mean that
Demonax was not prepared to die, or that he compromised his position. His defense was simply more convincing and hence superior to
that of Socrates. His speech was direct and forceful: "Men of Athens,
you see me ready with my garland: come, sacrifice me like your
former victim, for on that occasion your offering found no favour with
the gods!" (11).

The rest of the work consists primarily of Demonax's sayings, for
it is for his philosophical sayings that Lucian would praise him.
The treatise consists largely of these sayings, without comment from
Lucian. Supplying only brief transitional statements, Lucian allows
the reader to evaluate them.

Demonax's death is reported in such a way as to elicit praise. When
he was so old that he could no longer care for himself, he stopped
eating, and thereby "took leave of life in the same cheerful humour
that people he met always saw him in" (65). His end was thus consistent with his whole life. Lucian concludes by describing the tributes
paid to Demonax and by stating what his narrative has accomplished:

> To honour him, they did obeissance to the stone bench on which he
> used to rest when he was tired, and they put garlands on it; for they felt
> that even the stone on which he had been wont to sit was sacred.

Everybody attended his burial, especially the philosophers; indeed, it was they who took him on their shoulders and carried him to the tomb.

These are a very few things out of many which I might have mentioned, but they will suffice to give my readers a notion of the sort of man he was. (67)

Momigliano has shown the affinity of autobiography with biography, and, in this regard, *The Life of Josephus* is worthy of consideration.[22] If our thesis is correct—namely, that there is an identifiable type of laudatory biography into which each of the cited examples falls and with which the gospels may also be classified—then one might expect to find similar techniques and *topoi* in an autobiographical narrative such as this one by Josephus.

Josephus probably composed his autobiography as a defense against Justus, a rival historian who had maligned him (*Life* 336–40). The narrative certainly reads like a defense of his character from the beginning, where he states that he possesses an excellent family background and offers as proof his heritage from both parents' sides of the family. Of his mother's family he writes:

My family is no ignoble one, tracing its descent back to priestly ancestors. Different races base their claim to nobility on various grounds; with us a connexion with the priesthood is the hallmark of an illustrious line. Not only, however, were my ancestors priests, but they belonged to the first of the twenty-four courses—a peculiar distinction—and to the most eminent of its constituent camps. Moreover, on my mother's side I am of royal blood; for the posterity of Asamonaeus, from whom she sprang, for a very considerable period were kings, as well as high-priests, of our nation. (1–2)[23]

And of his father's family, he writes, "Distinguished as he was by his noble birth, my father Matthias was even more esteemed for his upright character, being among the most notable men in Jerusalem, our greatest city" (7).

Immediately after this, he recounts his education and early signs of excellence (*aretē*):

I made great progress in my education, gaining a reputation for an excellent memory and understanding. While still a mere boy, about fourteen years old, I won universal applause for my love of letters: insomuch that the chief priests and leading men of the city used constantly to come to me for precise information on some particular in our ordinance. At about the age of sixteen I determined to gain personal experience of the several sects into which our nation is divided. These, as I have frequently mentioned, are three in number—the first that of the Pharisees, the second that of the Sadducees, and the third that of the Essenes. I thought that, after a thorough investigation, I should be in a position to select the best. So I submitted myself to hard training and laborious exercises and passed through the three courses. (8–11)

After associating for three years with a man named Bannus "who dwelt in the wilderness," Josephus returned in his nineteenth year and subjected himself to Pharisaic rule.

The remainder of the autobiography consists largely of Josephus's actions (chronologically organized) while serving in his command in Galilee, before the siege of Jotapata. To this half year, according to H. St. J. Thackeray,[24] have been added "brief sketches of his youth in Palestine and his later years in Rome . . . as prologue and epilogue." Apparently, it is chiefly to this period that Justus had addressed his criticisms, hence Josephus's preoccupation in an autobiography with amplifying only one segment of his life. He punctuates his account with a defense of his conduct, including his sympathetic response (forgiveness mixed with just punishment) to his opponents, whom he consistently succeeds in eventually overcoming (see 84ff., 102–103, 110–11, 168, 262–64, 266, 304–308, and other passages). He describes himself as the innocent victim of those who envied his high station (see, for example, 80ff., 84–86, and 204). He states that he was a just and fair administrator, and the narrative documents his many virtues, including wisdom, self-restraint, courage, piety, and compassion. Josephus claims that his aim was to preserve the peace in Galilee (77), and he attributes the revolt against Rome by the Tiberians directly to the life and actions of his accuser (340ff.).

There is ample opportunity for the reader to compare Josephus's life and character with those of his adversaries (see 80ff., 134ff., and 191ff.). In each case, Josephus emerges as superior. In 204 and following, Josephus, having decided he had had enough of public life, informed his friends of his intention to vacate his present office. The account of the events leading to a reversal of this decision is representative of the epideictic nature of the whole treatise.

That night I beheld a marvellous vision in my dreams. I had retired to my couch, grieved and distraught by the tidings in the letter, then I thought that there stood by me one who said: "Cease, man, from thy sorrow of heart, let go all fear. That which grieves thee now will promote thee to greatness and felicity in all things. Not in these present trials only, but in many besides, will fortune attend thee. Fret not thyself then. Remember that thou must even battle with the Romans." Cheered by this dream-vision I arose, ready to descend into the plain. On my appearance, the whole crowd of Galilaeans, which included women and children, flung themselves on their faces and with tears implored me not to abandon them to their enemies nor, by my departure, leave their country exposed to the insolence of their foes. Finding entreaties unavailing, they sought with adjurations to coerce me to stay with them; bitterly inveighing against the people of Jerusalem for not allowing their country to remain in peace.

With these cries in my ears and the sight of the dejected crowd before my eyes, my resolution broke down and I was moved to compassion; I felt that it was right to face even manifest perils for so vast a multitude. So I consented to remain. . . . (208–12)

The treatise concludes with references to various honors bestowed upon Josephus, a personal reference to his own family, including references to the praiseworthiness of his wife, and references to his continued friendship with those in high places. Obviously, a reference to his death would have been inappropriate.

The final treatise to be discussed is Philostratus's *The Life of Apollonius of Tyana*. Although the date of this work is the third century A.D., its nature and its affinities with the gospels make *The Life of Apollonius of Tyana* an excellent prospect for the genre that has been identified.

Philostratus explains that the work was commissioned by the wife of Septimus Severus. His reason for writing has been accurately summarized by David Cartlidge and David Dungan: "just as Caracalla's architects built a shrine for Apollonios out of marble, one of his court rhetoricians built a temple out of words—for the same purpose, i.e., to celebrate Apollonius's God-like nature and inspire reverence for him."[25] Philostratus himself writes: "I feel I ought to do something about the widespread ignorance of Apollonios by accurately relating the times when he said or did something and the kinds of wisdom as a result of which he succeeded in being considered both supernatural and a divine being (*daimonios te kai theios*)."[26] This purpose, and the manner by which it is accomplished, is clearly epideictic.

Philostratus begins his treatment of Apollonius with *topoi* related to his background and birth. "The home of Apollonios, then, was Tyana, a Greek city in the land of the Cappadokians" (I. 4). The praise of his father is derived from the fact that he "came from an old family of the original settlers, richer than others there, although it was a wealthy country." Note the comparison. The praise of his mother is based on her having given birth to Apollonius. While pregnant, she is confronted with a vision of the Egyptian god Proteus, who confirms that he, in fact, is the child she carries. His birth is announced by swans who flapped their wings and honked and who had surrounded her while she was mysteriously sleeping alone in a meadow. The significance of the occasion is accented by a bolt of lightning which, at the precise time of his birth, "seemed to strike the earth and then bounce back upward into the air where it vanished." Philostratus then comments, "By this sign, the Gods, I believe, revealed and foretold that Apollonios would become superior to all things earthly, even drawing near to the Gods, and soon."[27] In true encomiastic fashion, these statements of illustrious background and the accounts of birth, including events preceding the subject's birth, help prepare the reader for Apollonius's career and accomplishments as an adult sage and healer.

These preliminary accounts continue with a statement on Apollonius's educational excellence as a youth. Unexcelled as a student of philosophy, Apollonius demonstrated at an early age a "good memory and power of concentration," and he could speak flawless "Attic Greek." So accomplished was he that "all eyes were constantly turned toward him . . . he was admired by the hour." Just as the young eagle remains in the nest with his parents until ready for flight, Apollonius remained with his teachers until, when of age, he too soared above them "like Pythagoras, being given 'wings' for it by Something Greater" (I. 7). Even when he was a youngster at one of the Asklepian temples, sayings were created about Apollonius: "Where are you running to? To see the boy?" (I. 8). These, and other related accounts, which display techniques of both amplification and comparison, perform the rhetorical tasks of preparing the audience for those qualities which characterize Apollonius's illustrious life.

Philostratus includes "all" of what Apollonius "said and did" in the form of a philosopher–healer's extended travelogue, a popular literary device. Apollonius travels from city to city (country to country) learning, teaching, and healing. Throughout these narratives, it is clear that Apollonius by comparison is second to none, including kings, peoples, demons, healers, or other religious–philosophical personages. Apollonius is superior to all he encounters.

The clearest example of the use of comparison in this work occurs in book VII, at which point Philostratus begins what has been called "The Martyrdom of Philosophers."[28] His introduction of this segment definitely places this work in the epideictic category.

> I am aware that the conduct of philosophers under despotism is the truest touchstone of their character, and am in favour of inquiring in what way one man displays more courage than another. And my argument also urges me to consider the point; for during the reign of Domitian Apollonius was beset by accusations and writs of information, the several origins and and sources and accounts of which I shall presently enlarge upon; and as I shall be under the necessity of specifying the language which he used and the role which he assumed, when he left the court after convicting the tyrant rather than being himself convicted, so *I must first of all enumerate all the feats of wise men in the presence of tyrants which I have found worthy of commemoration, and contrast them with the conduct of Apollonius.* (VII. 1)[29]

Cartlidge and Dungan have described accurately the literary effect of this section:

> First Philostratus lists other examples where philosophers have faced death at the hands of a tyrant, e.g., Zeno, Plato, Diogenes, Crates. Then he finds fault with each one in such a way as to show that, not only was Apollonios' bravery, wit, and power superior to theirs, but he also confronted a tyrant who ruled the whole world—not just some petty island king or ruler of an obscure country.[30]

Following these comparisons, Philostratus presents a detailed description of Apollonius's trial in which he emphasizes the high virtue of risking one's life for the true philosopher's way and Apollonius' belief that he will not die at the hands of the tyrant. Apollonius delivers a final speech and then disappears from the courtroom.

Philostratus presents several accounts of Apollonius's death, thereby allowing the reader to decide for himself or herself. He then concludes his treatise with accounts of appearances and dreams, all of which occur after Apollonius's death. That *The Life of Apollonius of Tyana* belongs to the laudatory biographical category within the epideictic classification is clearly demonstrable on the basis of the genre's shared conventions: *topoi*, literary techniques, and authorial intent.

SUMMARY

In conclusion, the examples discussed in this chapter illustrate the problems related to genre identification. The first is a proper identification of the genre. In the previous chapter, a literary genre was defined as a body of literature characterized by a common pattern of constituent elements and shared conventions. Genre identification is contingent upon the identification of these shared purposes, literary techniques, and *topoi* employed to produce a common pattern. Further, the common pattern in question is a particular type of *bios* pattern, whose presence in antiquity is evident in the works of Polybius, Cicero, Lucian, Cornelius Nepos, and Plutarch. The nearest one could come to the rhetorical basis for this *bios* type of literature are prescriptions related to the composition of the encomium. In fact, it is the encomium which most closely mirrors the common pattern evident in all of the examples offered in this chapter, a pattern composed of similar *topoi*, techniques and related purposes. Such an accumulation of data warrants the use of the term *encomium* as a more precise designation of the genre we have hitherto labeled laudatory biography.[31] The term encomium would indeed be appropriate provided the generic meaning is not confused with the literary exercise described by Marrou as so important for Greco–Roman educational systems. In its use outside the classroom the encomium was much more flexible and less restrictive than rhetorical rules permitted. The rhetorical traditions are thus valuable as aids in the reconstruction of the literary genre we are discussing. The label *encomium biography* does seem to describe appropriately and accurately the literary phenomenon in question.

The second problem concerns the apparent variety within the encomium biographical classification. As the examples illustrated, the *bios* pattern was employed in various ways by different authors. Indeed, a comparison of any of these works (with the possible exception of those of Isocrates and Xenophon) would yield almost as many differences as similarities. They have been referred to as encomium, apology, and funeral oration; and the subjects which emerge have been king, soldier, philosopher, statesman, and religious leader. Whether myth is involved or not, each pattern developed and its constituent parts have been so similar as to warrant the same generic classification. Each made use of the techniques of amplification and comparison in accordance with the author's design. Each employed traditions related to the life of the subject either in a pretense to relative completeness (from birth to death) or in part (emphasizing only a portion of the life of the subject), as deemed appropriate by the author.[32] Each sought to magnify those praiseworthy qualities, actions, and virtues of the hero considered appropriate by the author. And several of the heroes (Evagoras, Moses, Agesilaus, Agricola) have been considered by their authors worthy not only of honor but also of emulation. In addition, the basic organizational procedures prescribed in the rhetorical rules for the encomium have been followed (i.e., they are implicit) in each instance. It may be concluded, therefore, that there did exist a *bios* genre of considerable importance in antiquity, whose primary purpose was to present a portrait of a person in such a way as either to elicit praise from an audience or to persuade an audience of the subject's praiseworthiness. Thus the first of the criteria for a genre appropriate to the gospel narratives (referred to previously as basic observations; see pp. 36ff.), has been met: a *bios* narrative in which the person stands in the center of the literary stage.

The third problem is related to the function of preserving traditions for the good of the readers or even for total communities. This aspect is important if the gospels are to be classified within this literary type. Several of the works cited include statements to the effect that the author intends the literary portrait to be preserved for the good of posterity. For example, Isocrates writes, in *Evagoras* 4, "But the spoken words which should adequately recount the deeds of Evagoras would make his virtues never to be forgotten among all mankind." Tacitus writes (*Agricola* 1), "To hand down to posterity the works and ways of famous men was our fathers' custom," and,

> Whatever we have loved in Agricola, whatever we have admired, abides, and will abide, in the hearts of men, in the procession of the ages, in the records of history. Many of the Ancients has Forgetfulness engulfed. . . . Agricola, whose story here is told will outlive death, to be our children's heritage. (46)

Finally, consider Lucian's words (*Demonax* 2): "It is now fitting to tell of Demonax . . . that he may be retained in memory by men of culture . . . and that young men of good instincts who aspire to philosophy . . . may be able to set themselves a pattern from our modern world. . . ." Similar concerns are commonly expressed in the prologues of historians, and they provide one motive for the heroic epic. In each case, the emphasis upon preserving tradition for succeeding generations stands out, a practice common in the past and relevant for the present and future.[33] What is set forth and preserved for posterity in encomium biography is *bios* not history, character not recorded events. These portraits, therefore, although they may include traditions which are historical, are nevertheless not intended as history and are solely dependent upon the occasion, the audience, and the particular purposes of the individual authors. They are presented for approval—portraits which, if accepted, have moral implications for those who would shape their own character accordingly. This meets the second criterion for an appropriate genre for the gospels: the encomium biography consists of *bios* narratives of praise whose authors did not intend them as historical records.

Finally, in each of these examples, the authors were free to digress from the "norms" of *bios* writing in order to construct this pattern. Encomium biography often included material which was not prescribed by the rhetoricians, and this simply affirms our previous statement that genre determination cannot be reduced to "how-to-write" questions. The examples cited contained large amounts of such material. If, for example, Tacitus is permitted his interest in the geography of Britain and Isocrates his preoccupation with Theseus, then, without affecting the genre determination, Matthew may be granted his special christological concerns and any other materials which may have influenced the portrait of the person Jesus. In this respect, the encomium biographical genre may be viewed as a live option for a genre with which the gospels, with their cultic emphases, may be classified. This genre offers the possibility of accounting for the wholeness of the gospels as literary units while providing for the inclusion and development of their constituent parts. This possibility must now be tested, and it is to this task that we now turn.

4

The Relationship of Matthew to Biography

It is a trite but true observation that examples work more forcibly on the mind than precepts: and if this be just in what is odious and blameable, it is more strongly so in what is amiable and praiseworthy. . . . A good man therefore is a standing lesson to all his acquaintance, and of far greater use in that narrow circle than a good book. But as it often happens that the best men are but little known, and consequently cannot extend the usefulness of their examples a great way; the writer may be called into aid to spread their history farther, and to present the amiable pictures to those who have not the happiness of knowing the originals; and so, by communicating such valuable patterns to the world, he may perhaps do a more extensive service to mankind than the person whose life originally afforded the pattern. In this light I have always regarded those biographers who have recorded the actions of great and worthy persons of both sexes. . . . In all these, delight is mixed with instruction, and the reader is almost as much improved as entertained.[1]

Methodologically, the problem of the relationship of the gospels to the encomium genre is not easily addressed. The issue was skirted in the selection of the examples cited in the previous chapter but must now be considered. The frustrations of the obvious approach—a comparison of the gospel narratives with examples from antiquity on a one-to-one basis—have already been noted in our study of C. W. Votaw's work and K. L. Schmidt's response.[2] Such an approach suffers for several reasons.

First, it has been noted that, in a given genre, no two authors write for the same purpose or occasion. If there were an author who looked upon his or her literary hero in the same manner and wrote for precisely the same reasons as did the gospel writers, then perhaps such a one-to-one comparison could be set up, with the requisite controls for sound methodological results. But this is not the case even with the examples presented earlier for consideration. Even in works by the same author, the literary techniques of amplification and comparison were used in different ways, as was the particular *topoi* employed; and this is found to be true when each example is compared with the others.

Second, the dynamic aspect of genre, which presupposes literary flux, works against the notion of placing authorial creativity into fixed and arbitrary molds. For example, one of the gospels could be compared with Philo's *De vita Mosis*. This particular comparison would have the advantage that both works are of the same general period; both are about men of religious conviction acting according to divine design; both are apologetic in tone, each designed to present its subject favorably; and both indicate that the authors are loyal to their sources. Although these similarities suggest the relevance of such a comparison, without an acknowledged generic common denominator there would be considerable problems. In the first place, for example, Philo was seeking to elevate Moses in a Hellenistic society, whereas the gospel writers sought to enlist a faith response to the divine man to whom they bore witness. Second, one can be relatively certain of the way in which Philo has used his sources (Scriptures), and this provides some control over the assessment of Philo's method and approach. On the other hand, although the gospel writers depended on sources, the exact scope and nature of this material are still the object of critical inquiry. Nor is one able to assess clearly the relative abilities and skills of the respective authors. Apart from the common denominator of genre, there are simply too many variables and unknowns connected with the gospels and *bios* literature for comparisons on a one-to-one basis to be methodologically convincing. Methodologically, therefore, the problem is not to identify the "closest" example with which comparisons are to be made, but rather to demonstrate how the gospels are related to the common literary genre (the common denominator) which makes such comparisons methodologically valid. This methodology is based on the presupposition that the gospels do belong to the Greco–Roman milieu and can be so understood.

The more general question of the relationship of the gospels to the Greco–Roman world has been discussed by G. N. Stanton: "The main contention of this chapter is that, on the contrary, failure to read the gospels sufficiently carefully against the background of biographical writing in the ancient world has led to confused interpretations of their nature and intention."[3] Although Stanton stops short of positing conscious relationships, his conclusion in part supports some kind of direct affinities: "The gospels differ fundamentally from the biographical writing of the first centuries A.D., but, significantly for our purpose, the differences are least in evidence when the ways in which the character of a person was portrayed are considered."[4] The following discussion reveals that Stanton's conclusion is, in fact, an understatement.

One of the most impressive documents near-contemporary with the evangelists, which links the gospels with the "world of literature," is *Papyrus Oxyrhynchus* 1381, a document to which, until recently, only occasional reference has been made. The preface contains the story of the author and the divine task to which he is belatedly responding. Regrettably, only the preface has been preserved, but it must originally have been attached to a larger narrative devoted to the praise of the deity.

> However, as soon as Thou recognized, O Master, that I was neglecting Thy divine book (*theia biblos*), I invoked Thy providence and, being filled by Thy divinity (*theiotēs*) I eagerly hastened to the Heaven-sent prize of Thy narrative (*historia*). For I hope to make Thy intention widely known through my prophecy. In fact I have already written a plausible explanation of the story (*mythos*) of the creation of the world (by turning it into) natural concepts (*physikō logō*) closer to the truth.
>
> Throughout the writing I added what was lacking and removed what was superfluous so that I wrote briefly an overly wordy narrative (*diēgēma*) and told once a repetitive story (*allattologos mythos*). Accordingly, O Master, I deem the book to have been finally completed according to Thy kindness and not according to my intention. A writing (*graphē*) such as this suits Thy divinity, O Asklepios, for Thou hast disclosed it! Thou, greatest of Gods and Teacher, shalt be made known by the thanks of all people. For every gift of a votive offering or a sacrifice lasts only for a moment, and immediately perishes, while scripture (*graphē*) is an undying thanks (*athanatos charis*) since it rejuvenates the memory (of God's kindness) again and again. And every Greek tongue shall tell of Thy story (*historia*) and every Greek man shall worship Imouthes of Ptah.[5]

Scholars generally refer to this work as an aretalogy, though the exact form and structure of the treatise cannot be determined. The extant portion was written by a person obviously skilled in rhetoric who employed several terms which are important for the evangelists: *kērussō, dunamis, didaskalos,* and *apodidōmi,* in addition to *biblos* and *graphē.*[6] Of particular interest, furthermore, is the dedication of the author to his divine task and the editorial procedure he claims to have employed, both of which are evident in the above passage. Thus we encounter in the *Papyrus Oxyrhynchus* 1381 an educated author who shares both many of the concerns and some of the terminology of the evangelists. Here, as with the gospels, if to a lesser degree, the world of literature and the concerns of faith meet.

The absence of the "literary I," the personality of the author, has been used to argue against the kind of relationship we are affirming. Stanton responds to this argument by noting that the primary method of character portrayal is "the recognition that a person's actions and words sum up his character more adequately than the comments of an observer" [including an author].[7] Consequently, an author of antiquity would frequently be content to remain in the background, while the contents and arrangement of the traditions were combined to develop the portrait. For support, Stanton cites Xenophon, *Memorabilia* I. 3. 1; Isocrates, *Evagoras* 76; Xenophon, *Agesilaus* I. 6; and Plutarch, *Alexander*, I. 2; and, in addition, we have already seen Lucian adopt this procedure in his portrayal of Demonax. Stanton, therefore, cautiously concludes:

> This method of indirect characterisation, in which the personality of the author himself remained in the background, was a widely practised technique in ancient historiography generally. It is true, as R. Bultmann notes, that unlike Hellenistic biographies, the gospels do not let the personalities of their authors appear. But in sketching out a person's character, ancient writers were content to let the actions and words of their subject speak for themselves; at this point the gospels do not differ markedly.[8]

Theodore Weeden has argued on different grounds in his work on Mark, but the conclusion is the same. Agreeing that indirect characterization was common in ancient historiography, Weeden refers to the precedent set by Livy:

> Livy's view that the meaning of history is best seen in the people who act it out is well attested by the remarks addressed to his readers in the preface of his *Ab Urbe Condita.* . . . In drawing out this meaning of history through his characters, Livy rarely offers direct personal commentary on the ramifications of their lives. He chooses, rather, to provide such interpretation indirectly by the way in which he depicts and highlights traits and actions of his characters within the historical drama. . . . Often the effect which Livy wishes to create for the reader's judgment requires that he take serious liberties with historical personages: reshaping, redirecting, in fact rewriting their lives to meet his own

needs. The concern for historical accuracy is set aside. The heroes are idealized. The villains are denigrated. For Livy, this is not misrepresentation of history but its proper interpretation.[9]

Weeden concludes his analysis by stating that there is no reason the author of Mark could not have adopted a similar indirect method of presenting his narrative. Of course, the same is true of each canonical gospel.

It would appear, therefore, that the relationship of the gospels to the encomium biographical genre is not as farfetched a notion as has been hitherto believed. The gospels belong to the milieu of the Greco–Roman world, and the methodological basis for comparisons is dependent upon a common genre. As Schmidt and others have observed, the gospels and their writers may fall short of "high" literary endeavors. They may, indeed, be less educated as authors, and their work less self-conscious; but the pattern which they developed and presented is similar in many ways to the ubiquitous pattern found in laudatory biography of antiquity. The dramatic nature of their narratives argues for a relationship that is more than accidental—natural, because of the ubiquity of the pattern, but certainly not altogether accidental.[10]

It is now appropriate to test this hypothesis by examining Matthew's gospel in relation to encomium biography. This examination necessarily involves an analysis of the conventions, *topoi,* literary technique, and authorial intent.[11] Matthew has been chosen as the test case because it has received the least attention by those who would relate the gospels to Greco–Roman literature.[12] Also, a discussion of the genre of Matthew would be equally relevant under any source hypothesis.[13] The presupposition is that Matthew is a single literary whole, regardless of the fact that its pattern was developed primarily by collecting and editing and regardless of the position it occupies in the chronological sequence of "gospel" literature. The purpose of the analysis is to make sense of Matthew against the background of encomium biography.

THE GOSPEL OF MATTHEW

Topoi

Matthew begins his work with Jesus' family background. This includes not only his father and mother, but also those genealogical relationships with significant figures of his Jewish heritage. It is the presentation of this *topos* which constitutes the precise beginning of the gospel as a literary unit.[14] In Matt. 1:1, Jesus is described as the "son of David" and the "son of Abraham," the former identification being especially important for messianic expectation and the latter being indicative of God's promise. The genealogy that follows validates these emphases. Its structure is set forth in v. 17, where Matthew notes that fourteen generations separate Abraham from David, David from the deportation, and the deportation from Jesus, although there are, in fact, only thirteen names in the last section. This structure reflects how the attempt to make a theological point can dictate the structure (if not the historical accuracy) of the genealogy, an observation that is consistent with the unhistorical nature of the gospel as a whole. The number fourteen is a plenary one, as is Philo's "seven" in his account of the generations from Abraham to Moses (*De vita Mosis*, 11. 7). Matthew's genealogy includes four women, thereby anticipating the "holy irregularity" evident in tracing the lineage of Jesus through the husband of the virgin Mary.[15] God's promise is fulfilled through a woman, just as in the past. This genealogy, which builds to Jesus' birth, calls one's attention to the significance, and anticpates the accomplishments, of the person with whom the whole gospel is concerned. It authenticates the identity of Jesus and makes viable subsequent identifications of Jesus with the Messiah (e.g., 16:13ff.). The genealogy, therefore, is part of Matthew's preparation for his portrait of Jesus' adult role.

The next pericope describes Joseph's response to Mary's pregnancy before their marriage (1: 18–25). Mary's conception out of wedlock augurs the miraculous advent of the Messiah. It is the fourteenth generation of the third epoch, and messianic hope is fulfilled in the womb of a virgin. What appears strange in his presentation is the prominance of Joseph in Matthew's narrative. Joseph emerges as the central character in vv. 18–25. Joseph's presence verifies Jesus' "legal descent" from David, whereas the real father is God, according to dream revelation. Matthew further focuses upon Joseph by referring to him as a "just man" (*dikaios*), a qualitative judgment substantiated by his discussion of divorce—a problem Joseph faces when he learns Mary is pregnant. Only Jesus is called *dikaios* elsewhere in Matthew's narrative (27:19), which reveals the significance of Jesus' earthly father in Matthew's eyes. Chapter 1, therefore, makes four important points: (1) it indicates clearly the precise time of God's fulfillment of his promise with Jesus' birth; (2) it traces Jesus' genealogy through Joseph by way of his virgin mother, Mary; (3) it specifically identifies the upright character of his earthly and "legal" father by calling him a just or righteous man; and (4) it prefaces Jesus' birth with an act of God (dream). It will be recalled that each of these points coincides with the *topoi* commonly found in examples of encomium literature. For the relationship of the fourth *topos* to birth, see Cicero (*De Partitione Oratoria* XXIII. 82) and especially Hermogenes, who writes, "You will say what marvelous things befell at his birth, as dreams, signs or the like."[16]

Chapter 2 consists of the stories of the Magi, the slaughter of the innocents, the flight into Egypt, and the settlement of the holy family in Nazareth. It is not necessary here to deal with each story individually. One notes the relationship between these events in Jesus' early life and in that of Moses, as reported in the book of Exodus. It is quite possible that Matthew intended for some of his readers to make this soteriological identification, in which case Jesus' life also depicts God's saving activity. There are parallels to the slaughter of the innocents in Hellenistic literature, as well as in the life of Moses,[17] which reveals more about the popularity of the theme than about Matthew's source. Great people often are reported to have escaped premature death. The influence of the supernatural (the star[18] guiding the Magi and the instructions to the holy family in a dream) and the hero's deliverance from a premature death are ingredients previously encountered in the encomium biography.[19] The essential problem of the chapter has been properly identified as the need to reconcile the traditions about Jesus' birth in Bethlehem and those about his being from Nazareth. The dream is significant in the development of the chapter. Because of the danger of living under Herod, Joseph is instructed in a dream to flee to Egypt. After Herod's death, the family returns to Nazareth (again instructed by God in a dream). In this way, every prophecy is fulfilled (e.g., Matt. 2:5, 15, 17, 23). The preliminary events by which Matthew prepares his readers for the adult Jesus include the illustrious lineage of Jesus through his earthly father, his miraculous birth, his upright earthly father, the time and place of his birth, his escape from death as an infant,[20] and his hometown—*topoi* which are accented by dreams, stellar illumination, and the adoration of the child. Such preliminary procedures serve as mere indicators of the greatness yet to be described when Jesus comes of age. It is evident that, through chapter 2, Matthew's gospel excludes neither Jew nor Gentile, and these chapters qualify as a good example of the manner in which the ancients praised their heroes.

The issues in chapter 3 are the baptism of Jesus and the person and work of John the Baptist. John is clearly identified with Elijah, and is thus a forerunner of the Messiah. The real climax of the story is the baptism, performed at Jesus' insistence, followed by a theophany in which the spirit of God descends in the form of a dove and alights on Jesus. The whole episode seems to depict the empowering of Jesus by God's spirit; and the voice from heaven says, "This is my beloved Son. . . ." In many ways, this chapter constitutes the beginning of Jesus' ministry. The problematic gap between the settlement of Jesus and his family in Nazareth and the advent of John supports this interpretation. From a literary point of view, however, one can see that Matthew is continuing a trend of thought begun in chapter 1, which will not be broken until the beginning proper of Jesus' ministry (4:12). In chapter 1, Jesus is identified as the "son of David." In chapter 2, Herod fears that he is a threat to his own throne, that is, he misunderstood the implications of messianic kingship. In chapter 3, Jesus' identity has been disclosed in terms of divine sonship, and in chapter 4, vv. 1–11, this identity is the occasion for the temptation (see vv. 3 and 6). Thus, in the context of the encomium biography, all of Matt. 1–4:11 constitutes a preliminary section in which the evangelist clearly defines Jesus' identity and early signs of greatness. In this way, Matthew has prepared his readers for the full impact and authority of Jesus' ministry, which is to occupy the major section of his gospel. This literary procedure, as previously noted, is in common with what has been identified as the encomium genre.[21] The accounts of Jesus' baptism and temptation are substitutes for stories about the excellences of his early childhood and youth, and these themes are far more appropriate in Matthew's narrative, given the religious nature of the subject, than they would be in other such accounts which praise kings, philosophers, and statesmen.

In Matthew, the temptation account is closely related to the baptism; and it is the Spirit who leads Jesus into the wilderness. Satan, the tempter, is fully aware of Jesus' identity as the "Son of God" (4:3

and 6). There are three specific temptations, two of which are prefaced with "if you are the Son of God. . . ." The conditional "if" serves as a challenge to Jesus to assert his messianic power on his own terms, a challenge to which Jesus in each instance does not succumb. Furthermore, through his resistance, Jesus shows himself to be superior to Satan's onslaught, and he retains this superiority throughout Matthew's narrative. Whatever else one may say of Matthew's temptation account, it is apparent that Jesus is presented as a messianic figure of obvious moral strength, capable both of withstanding temptation and of giving spiritual and scriptural leadership. As Birger Gerhardsson notes, "Jesus was tempted in everything, as we are, yet he was without sin."[22] We have encountered others in encomium biographical literature who were praised because their vocational choices were not altered by other tempting possibilities (for example, Agricola resisted fame, Moses, his royal inheritance in Egypt, and Demonax, wealth). In each case, Jesus included, the allegiance to higher aims and responsibilities is indeed commendable and authenticating. It is precisely at this point in the narrative that Matthew turns to the account of Jesus' ministry.

The final group of *topoi* to be considered are those surrounding Jesus' death. Specific references to Jesus' impending death began in Matthew's gospel as early as 16:21. Three additional predictions follow before his death is actually reported. These initial observations demonstrate the importance of Jesus' death to the tradition and the importance of the event for Matthew. Our concern is particularly with the manner in which Matthew specifically develops his account and what accompanies it.

Jesus' death is attributed to a plot by his opponents.[23] In Matt. 26:3–5, the chief priests and the elders take counsel against him, in order "to arrest Jesus by stealth and kill him." They again take counsel in Matt. 27:1, and Matthew repeats the sinister design, "to put him to death." Following the arrest, Matthew includes the story of the repentance and death of Judas (27:3–10), which has been properly called an etiological tale[24] to which has been added the theme of fulfillment.[25] From a literary point of view, this special treatment by Matthew reflects upon Jesus' character and innocence, showing that his own betrayer, realizing his mistake, attempted unsuccessfully to rectify it.

Supernatural events surround Jesus' death just as they did his birth. Matthew's account emphasizes this at several notable points. Pilate, for example, is warned to have nothing to do with Jesus, who is described as a "righteous man."[26] This warning is issued by Pilate's wife as the result of a *dream* (27:19).[27] Matthew includes references to the darkness over the land at the time of Jesus' death (27:45) and to the damage to the curtain in the temple (27:51). Matthew then adds: "the earth shook, and the rocks were split; the tombs also were opened, and many bodies of the saints who had fallen asleep were raised, and coming out of the tombs after his resurrection they went into the holy city and appeared to many" (27:51b–53). This reference to the earthquake and the additional phenomena of resurrection and appearance is, in Matthew, related specifically to Jesus' death, though a portion of the text obviously refers to Jesus' resurrection. Matthew reports a second earthquake on the first day of the week as a preface to the descent of an angel, whose appearance is like lightning and whose raiment is white as snow. Regardless of the precise interpretation one chooses to adopt, all of these events are remarkable literary testimony to the significance of Jesus' death in accordance with God's design and the magnificence of the resurrection by which Jesus is glorified.

Jesus' death also provides the occasion for Matthew to elaborate on his innocence. The repentance and suicide of Judas have already been mentioned. Further, the dream of Pilate's wife anticipates the Matthean account in which Pilate washes his hands of the guilt of Jesus' blood (27:24–26), a statement of his personal view that Jesus was innocent of the charges. In addition, not only did the centurion and others witness the damage to the temple (Matt. 27:51), in Matthew they saw additional signs and responded in unison: "Truly this was a son of God!" (see Matt. 27:54).[28] Even in death, therefore, Jesus is vindicated.

Finally, Matthew gives special evidence of the resurrection. In Matt. 27:63ff., Pilate establishes a guard to prevent the theft of Jesus' body and to squelch all possible rumors of a resurrection. Shortly thereafter (28:4), it is the soldiers themselves who witness the gloriously adorned angel rolling the stone away from the tomb, and their response is one of extreme fear. Still later (28:11–15), the soldiers are bribed and instructed to change their testimony to accuse the disciples of having stolen the body. No doubt these events are recorded to

counter the attack on the resurrection event during the evangelist's
time. As Bultmann has noted:

> If is further possible to reckon among the faith legends those that are
> due to *apologetic motives*: . . . the stories about the sepulchre guards
> Matt. 27:62–66, 28:11–15, and a number of small features in the Passion
> narrative. . . .[29]

Consequently, Matthew's readers can trust in the resurrection, on
account not only of the empty tomb but also of the direct testimony
from the guards who were commissioned by the Jewish authorities
and who witnessed the event. In a striking way, then, Matthew employs Jesus' judge as proof of his innocence, his betrayer as testimony
to the truth of Jesus' ministry and mission, the centurion and others
as witness to his divine sonship (confirmed in the face of his humiliation), the soldiers posted at the tomb at the insistence of his enemies
as proof of his resurrection, and natural phenomena as evidence for
the significance of the events in relation to God's action—an exquisite
apologia. Thus, by elaboration and amplification, Matthew trans-
forms, for his readers, the lowliest form of death in the Greco–Roman
period into a victorious glorification of Jesus, a literary task equal in
artistry to an encomium biography. A humiliating death has been so
presented as to elicit both praise and faith from the reader.

Techniques

There are several general observations to be made about Matthew's
literary techniques. He does not attempt to trace chronologically
Jesus' life; but rather he uses the *bios* form as an outline through
which to organize the traditions which commend Jesus. Matthew's
geographical references serve the author's design, not history's purposes. Accordingly, Matthew provides the literary "historical" context for traditions which would otherwise have no such context, and
thereby veils his intended meanings with the character of history.
This method is similar to that of Tacitus's *Agricola*, in which his apologetic is veiled in a conquest of Britain without a real concern for
geographical accuracy. In both instances, the traditions which eulogize the hero are "historicized" (for example, one should note the
incorporation of Jesus' Sermon on the Mount and the speeches of
Calgacus and Agricola in *Agricola* 29–36). Matthew further validates

his narrative with numerous Old Testament quotations, each of which is introduced with the relatively fixed formula quotation clauses (e.g., 1:22; 2:15; 17, 23, and so on). In a similar though not conclusive manner, Plutarch's "Lives" (*bioi*) incorporate quotations from ancient poets to support the praiseworthiness of his subjects (*Philopoemen* XI. 2–3, and *Aristides* III. 4). In addition, Matthew displays a preference for thematically organized collections of material. For example, the Sermon on the Mount (Matt. 5–7) concerns righteousness, the mission charge (chap. 10) focuses upon the costs of discipleship, the parabolic materials in chapter 13 are about the kingdom and its growth, the church's disciplines are collected in chapter 18, and teachings about the Pharisees, *parousia*, and the Last Judgment are collected in chapters 23 through 25. A stereotypical phrase concludes each of these collected units (7:28; 11:1; 13:53; 19:1; and 26:1). In addition, Matthew 8 and 9 consist of a collection of miracle stories into which the evangelist incorporates his concern for discipleship (hence, the insertion of the sayings of 8:18–19 and the repeated references to "faith," in 8:10, 26; 9:2, and so on). The organization of collected traditions which convey specific emphases and virtues was also encountered in Philo's *De vita Mosis* and Xenophon's *Agesilaus* and is also evident in Suetonius's *Deified Julius*. It is clear that each of these Matthean techniques was also commonly employed in Greco–Roman literature related to the encomium biography.

Both the literary techniques of amplification and comparison, which were specifically isolated for discussion as conventions of the encomium biography, have also been employed by Matthew. The emphasis upon the progressive disclosure of Jesus' identity (Matt. 1–4:11), in lieu of the early childhood and educational events, is one example of amplification. A second is the treatment of the *topoi* surrounding Jesus' death. Both sections are heightened by the use of dreams, supernatural phenomena, and the additional testimony of eyewitnesses, which clearly indicates the use of this technique in the light of Matthew's purposes. In addition to these two examples, which have been discussed previously in a different context, the use of amplification is evidenced by the particular portions of Jesus' life chosen by Matthew for presentation. As with Josephus's autobiographical account, a relatively small segment has been selected, namely, the preliminary traditions about the birth and the beginning of the ministry per se, the ministry itself, which focuses on only a relatively small portion of Jesus' life in comparison with the report of his passion, and the accounts of his death and the subsequent events in his glorification. These few highlights would hardly qualify the end result as a complete "life" in modern terms, but they are most certainly adequate for the portrait Matthew wishes to paint. In this respect, the gospel of Matthew does not differ markedly from other lives of the same period. After all, from these concentrated traditions, one can well discern the identity projected, the message proclaimed and the actions performed, the nature of the opposition Matthew offers as the reason for Jesus' death, and the actions and purposes of God throughout the entire process. In other words, these are the traditions Matthew has decided to amplify in his narrative in order to accomplish his particular ends; and the implicit literary decisions are well within the scope of and possess the characteristics of the encomium genre. The same type of decisions must have been made, for example, in Josephus's autobiography[30] and in Philo's *De vita Mosis*,[31] and they are implied in Plutarch's preface to his life of Alexander.[32] Indeed, a similar preface would have been appropriate for Matthew's narrative. Rather than making a viable case for excluding his gospel from *bios* literature, the limited scope of Matthew's narrative supports its inclusion within the encomium biographical genre, when the use of amplification, a technique in which incompleteness serves the author's purposes, is taken into account. If this technique is taken seriously by New Testament critics, it calls into question, if it does not completely remove from the arena of the synoptic problem, arguments based solely upon the omission of tradition.[33]

Matthew's use of comparison is even more apparent. In chapter 3, Matthew presents the traditions which convey the relationship between Jesus and John the Baptist (previously discussed in connection with Jesus' baptism). It is apparent from the traditions of John the Baptist as preserved in all of the gospels and Acts that John was an important figure in his own right, that he both preached and baptized, and that he attracted a following of disciples. What is important for present considerations is the manner in which Matthew structures these traditions which depict the relationship of Jesus to John. To begin with, he presents the tradition of John as a voice in the wilderness preparing the way of the Lord. Matthew presents the content of

John's preaching as being identical with that of Jesus (see Matt. 3:2 and 4:17); he also identifies the group coming for baptism in Matt. 3:7 as the Pharisees and Sadduccees. Thus he draws a parallel between the message and opponents of Jesus and the message and opponents of John.[34] This may mislead the reader into considering that Jesus has become John's disciple through baptism. The conversation between Jesus and John immediately preceding Jesus' baptism clarifies their relationship. John's hesitation to baptize him and his testimony in which he reveals his willingness to be baptized by Jesus clearly eliminate the possibility of his followers' claiming supremacy over Jesus or even equality with him. In fact, John's significance, through his identification with Elijah, enhances Jesus' importance for the reader: John is indeed one preparing the way for another *greater* than he. Following the baptism, the heavenly voice and the descent of the dove confirm this conclusion and emphasize the precise role of each. In Matthew, John is arrested before Jesus' ministry begins, presumably to dispel any remaining confusion. Therefore, secondary to the empowering of Jesus by the Spirit is the critical literary affirmation that, since John can be considered great, how much greater is Jesus.

Matthew's depiction of Jesus' relationship with his opponents also reveals his use of comparison. The initial indications of opposition are only implied. The first appears at the conclusion of the Sermon on the Mount: "And when Jesus finished these sayings, the crowds were astonished at his teaching, for he taught them as one who had authority, and not as their scribes" (7:28–29). The reference is obviously to the superiority of Jesus' authority to that of the scribes, and, though unstated, the seeds of envy have been planted. The second indication appears in 9:11, when the Pharisees ask Jesus' disciples, "Why does your teacher eat with tax collectors and sinners?" Jesus offers a general response, and it is as though the Pharisees are not even present to hear it. In 9:34, Matthew adds the comment that Jesus is casting out demons by the prince of demons, a charge leveled by the Pharisees. To this charge, Jesus makes no reply, although he does in 12:22ff., where the same charge is made. The fourth preliminary reference is in chapter 10, where Jesus warns his disciples, whom he has just commissioned to go to the house of Israel (10:6), of the opposition they will encounter (10:16–25). It is apparent that the rejection his disciples will encounter will be the same as that which

Jesus himself is about to experience. Thus, prior to Matt. 12:1 and the episode of picking grain on the Sabbath, the opposition to Jesus is suppressed, and direct conflict is avoided in favor of developing the reader's anticipation.

The conflict stories are presented more directly and intensely, beginning with 12:1ff. Jesus is confronted directly when his disciples pluck grain on the Sabbath, and he is challenged when he heals the man with the withered arm (12:1–13). The second pericope concludes with the first reference to the plot against Jesus' life: "But the Pharisees went out and took counsel against him, how to destroy him" (v. 14). There are two additional conflict stories in chapter 12, and the reader is now aware that the opposition to Jesus is both overt and sinister. His superiority is apparent in these conflict narratives: since his opponents are incapable of defeating him, they must destroy him.

The conflict narratives again become concentrated in chapter 21 and build to a climax in 22:45. Matthew's account is clear: for the first time Jesus is depicted as the aggressor, following a series of confrontations initiated by his opponents, as he asks the Pharisees a question they choose not to answer. Matthew describes the response: "And no one was able to answer him a word. . . ." (22:46a). Then follows the statement: ". . . nor from that day did any one dare to ask him any more questions" (22:46b). Thus, in Matthew, whereas Jesus answered all of his opponents' charges and questions, they were at a loss to answer his challenge. The reader, therefore, concludes that Jesus is superior to his opponents, a situation which is only resolved, for them, by his eventual suffering and death. Matthew sets up the comparison between Jesus and his opponents in a progressive way: there is an initial phase of impending conflict; a phase of direct conflict, during which both sides are actively engaged (Jesus primarily defensively); and the climax, at which point Jesus' superiority is made so evident as to preclude any further relations between Jesus and his opponents. One is reminded of the envy encountered by Moses prior to his first flight from Egypt, the envy attributed to the opponents of Josephus, and the envy successfully avoided by the humble actions of Agricola which accounted for his longevity. In fact, according to Matthew, it is Pilate who recognizes that Jesus stands before him for judgment because of envy (27:18), which must have been generated in part by the conflicts cited above. Matthew's dramatic treatment of the conflict narratives and the eventual victory of his main character is consistent with what one might expect from an author whose hero is glorified by God's act of resurrection after an unjust and degrading death.

What is true of John the Baptist and Jesus' opponents is also true of all other personages in Matthew's gospel. Whether their actions are commendable or degrading, Matthew's characters direct one's attention to the central character, Jesus. At no point do Jesus' disciples surpass him, just as none of Apollonius of Tyana's followers surpass him. Matthew uses the other characters to voice opinions he wishes to be heard; the warning of Pilate's wife establishes her opinion that Jesus is a "righteous man" (27:19), the centurion and others together testify to the fact that this man was a son of God (27:54ff.), and the account of Judas' committing suicide is Matthew's way of saying that Jesus' death was unjustified. To these may be added the impression Jesus made on Pilate: "But he gave him no answer, not even to a single charge; so that the governor wondered greatly." (Matt. 27:14), and Pilate's symbolic attempt to rid himself of the responsibility of the crucifixion by washing his hands (27:24ff.). These techniques are comparable to Isocrates' use of Theseus to praise Helen and Philo's citing the positive opinion of all nations about Jewish law, which adds to the stature of the lawmaker, Moses.[35] More important, the technique of comparison, as illustrated in this discussion, demonstrates the affinity of the gospel of Matthew with those narratives composed in antiquity for the presentation and praise of a historical *bios*. It is now apparent that Matthew uses amplification and comparison just as they are used in the examples of encomium biographies cited in the previous chapter.

Purpose

A sufficient amount of Matthew's text has been examined to allow for at least two preliminary conclusions regarding the author's intent. First, Matthew intends to state clearly the identity of Jesus as the "Son of God." The importance of this identification for Matthew is clear from the key positions it occupies in the text, for it is the title to which the first four chapters build. The authentication of this identity by numerous references to the Old Testament prophecies understood to be related to "the one who is to come" confirm for the reader the messianic identity of the person about whom the narrative has been written. The question asked of Peter in chapter 16, "But who do you say that I am?" (v. 15), is asked of everyone who reads Matthew, and the appropriate answer is that of Peter, "You are the Christ, the Son of the living God" (v. 16).

Matthew is aware, however, that the proper response is contingent upon the portrait he develops. With what must have been considerable care, Matthew responds to his reader's expectations. Jesus is indeed of Davidic lineage and has initiated God's kingdom according to God's design and activity. He is king, but one whose kingdom could never really threaten Herod's earthly throne. He is, rather, the king whose exaltation comes after his humiliation: the victorious hero is the innocent one who suffers a degrading death.

Matthew's concern includes the recognition of Jesus' messianic activity. After completing the preliminary accounts (4:11), Matthew reports John's arrest, prophetic fulfillment, the content of Jesus' preaching, and the calling of disciples, all of which appear to be necessary before the details of Jesus' ministry can be presented. These pericopes are concisely written and loosely strung together. Verse 23 describes Jesus' activity: "And he went about all Galilee, teaching in their synagogues and preaching the gospel of the kingdom and healing every disease and every infirmity among the people." There follows a list of the diseases and infirmities he healed. In reality, Matt. 4:23ff. serves as a programmatic statement which introduces both the Sermon on the Mount (chaps. 5–7) and the miracles of chapters 8–9 (note the healings listed in 4:24 compared with those in chaps. 8–9), a programmatic statement which summarizes Jesus' messianic activity. The proper response to this messianic activity is evident in the one who hears and does as Jesus proclaims, thereby building his life on a sure foundation of righteousness (7:24ff.). Faith is the key to living amid all manner of adversity (chaps. 8–9), and again the basis for faith in Matthew's eyes is the testimony to Jesus' words and deeds ("Go and tell John what you hear and see." 11:4). Thus Matthew has placed into literary balance the continuity of Jesus' messianic identity and activity: identity in 1–4:11 and activity in 5–9. Matthew's purpose, therefore, is to present a convincing portrait of the crucified and risen Messiah, whose identity and activity on earth elicit faith from both those in the story and the reader of the narrative.

The second purpose which may be attributed to Matthew from the previous discussions is to inspire emulation of the Messiah's activity. Chapters 1–9 constitute a paradigm of discipleship. There is no direct conflict during this period because, for Matthew, this period of Jesus' activity is identical with the period of the reader who is being taught and trained prior to being "sent" (chap. 10). Matthew's literary design is *didactic*, intended to instruct the true disciple of the church. Such a conclusion is warranted by the following observations. Having stated clearly Jesus' identity, Matthew presents Jesus' teaching in the Sermon on the Mount, the most extensive collection of sayings material in Matthew's gospel, and the closest parallel one has to the presentation of teaching materials such as those preserved in Lucian's *Demonax*. Whereas the content of Jesus' message is important for his readers, Matthew proceeds to instruct them in the true nature of discipleship by his collection of miracles in chapters 8–9. Only after such instruction is the disciple ready for commissioning (chap. 10), which necessarily includes additional instruction in what the true, newly commissioned disciple can expect from those unbelievers who witness his words and deeds. We noted earlier that it was only afterwards that Jesus himself encountered directly the opposition that eventually led to his death. It is striking, therefore, that the disciple is told of impending trials *before* he is presented with an example with which he may identify. The model for facing opposition then unfolds in the person of Jesus (chaps. 12–28). Matthew's gospel, therefore, portrays the paradigm of the Christian life: acceptance of Jesus Christ as the Son of God, instruction in his words and deeds which elicits faith, testifying to the same by emulating Jesus' ministry of word and deed, and the assurance that the fate on earth of the true disciple is the fate of Jesus' humiliation and exaltation (chaps. 12–28).

Authorial purposes related to the hero's prominent identity, the significance of the hero's words and deeds, and the reader's response of emulation are common features of encomium biography and are to be found in Matthew's work. The nearest parallels are works of Philo (*De vita Mosis*), Lucian (*Demonax*), and Philostratus (*The Life of Apollonius of Tyana*), which we have discussed. The major difference is the evangelistic concern of the author. Although the apologetic tone may be present in Matthew, the reader's response of faith and the *didactic* instruction of his community are more important.

What Matthew desires from his audience is indeed praise of Jesus; but, even more important to him is this faith response. The *topoi* and techniques he has used are designed to elicit this response and to instruct the believer in the course he or she is to follow. The least one can say about the literary results is that Matthew's gospel reflects the conventions, *topoi*, and purposes of the encomium biographical genre. It is a *bios*, and it is more than a *bios*. The fact that the milieu of this gospel is both Greco–Roman and Jewish and the fact that Matthew has made use of a popular literary genre account for its reception and continued preservation.

Conclusion

There is a certain kind of penmanship made in schools which seems to draw around the letters of a word like a wire, and there is another penmanship, much more human, that seems to be the word.[1]

Through the course of this study, three aspects of the question of gospel genre have been explored: the statement of the problem, the identification of an appropriate solution, and an examination of one of the gospels, Matthew, in connection with the proposed solution.

The statement of the problem consisted of an examination of the major contributions to the question during the past seventy years by scholars such as C. W. Votaw, Karl Ludwig Schmidt, Martin Dibelius, Rudolph Bultmann, and Helmut Koester who shares his views, Moses Hadas and Morton Smith, and, more recent, Charles Talbert. Whereas Votaw felt free to make comparisons with ancient biographical works, the *sui generis* position of Schmidt, Dibelius, Bultmann, and Koester precluded such comparative studies until Hadas and Smith's work on aretalogy and Talbert's work on the mythic nature of both ancient biographical and gospel narratives. Because of the problems with the *sui generis* positions and problems with the proposed solutions related to aretalogy and myth, the conclusion was that the question until now has remained unanswered.

The solution to the question was introduced with a brief discussion of genre. The concept of genre was shown to be dynamic; that is, it refers to a general type in which there are many forms and variables involving purpose, *topoi,* and techniques. There is no "pure" form, but there are works which are considered models because they have exerted an influence on later works. Essential to a given genre is the pattern which emerges from the author's intentional use of *topoi* and literary conventions and the reason for which the pattern has been developed. Thus, Polybius can distinguish two distinct literary genres when writing of Philopoemen—one in which the pattern is to be included in a historical treatise and the other in which the pattern is intended to praise or persuade.

The preliminary identification of a genre in which the gospels could be classified was proposed by extracts from Polybius, Cicero, Cornelius Nepos, Plutarch, and Lucian. This genre was then given a more precise definition by turning to the prescriptive literary procedures evident in the educational system in the Greco–Roman world. Noticeably absent from this general type of literature was a single, predominant name by which a treatise therein could be identified, an observation which is not surprising given that biography was in an infant stage of development at the time the gospels were written. Whereas antiquity was relatively clear about what "history" should be, the recording of the lives of men exhibited considerable variety. It is certain that there was a type of biography designed to praise, honor, and defend; and, because this common type is clearly seen in the rhetorical descriptions of the literary exercise, encomium, the title "encomium biography" was supplied, for lack of a better term. Integral to this type of literature were *topoi* relevant to the praise of an individual, the literary techniques of comparison and amplification, and the author's intent to praise, commend, defend, or recommend for emulation. These conventions provided the author with the suitable tools and with the freedom to develop the particulars of his *bios* pattern in relation to his audience and occasioned purposes. Finally, conclusive confirmation of this genre was offered by presenting examples from antiquity which contained the encomium biography's shared conventions—"lives" by Isocrates, Xenophon, Philo, Tacitus, Lucian, Josephus, and Philostratus. There were many ways in which the individual treatises cited differed from one another, but each one reflected the *bios* pattern created through the use of shared *topoi*, literary techniques, and the purposes of praise, commendation, and vindication.

The third aspect was consideration of one of the gospels in relation to the shared conventions identified with *encomium biography*. The examination of the text of Matthew's gospel revealed a striking number of affinities with the encomium biographical genre and its shared conventions—enough to justify Matthew's classification within this genre. In the encomium biography, Matthew either consciously or unconsciously appropriated a ubiquitous literary type sufficiently flexible to carry out his designs of faith and emulation and to project his kerygmatic assertions within the cult (church) to be used for worship and didactic functions.

Assuming the validity of this study and its conclusions, one can now begin to ask if the remaining canonical gospels are also examples of encomium biography. Whereas, admittedly, the limited scope of the present work does not warrant such an immediate conclusion, the present study does bring the possibility to the point of serious consideration. One can hardly deny to Mark, Luke, and John, for example, Matthew's focus upon the *bios* of Jesus. Furthermore, even a cursory reading of these three gospels suggests that the biographical patterns employ *topoi*, techniques, and purposes similar to those employed in encomium biography. Firm conclusions, however, must await the results of more extensive research.

What is the genre of Matthew? Matthew belongs to that form of laudatory biography which can be identified as the encomium biography genre, and there is no longer any need either to qualify or to apologize for the use of the word *biography*. Too long has the justifiable reaction to the nineteenth-century *leben–Jesu–forschung* clouded the vision of gospel critics to the real nature of the biographical emphasis contained within Matthew's gospel. The Gospel According to Matthew contains traditions that are historical and even biographical, but the whole literary portrait developed by Matthew is not biographical in any modern sense of the term, and this gospel cannot be relied upon for such historical information as chronology, development, or appearance. Rather, it was primarily designed, among other things, to elicit faith and emulation—it was written by an evangelist. The book of Matthew as literature, however, stands within an ancient and respected tradition of literature which has been specifically designed for the purpose of praising the hero in a biographical composition. This means that the evangelist was not irresponsible in his tasks, nor is he to be faulted for the information we are unable to glean from the narrative. On the contrary, Matthew, for example, may now be seen as an author of literary integrity and the gospel as reflective of an attempt to relate the author's message to the society in which he lived.

Notes

CHAPTER 1—THE PROBLEM
UNDER CONSIDERATION

1. Ralph Waldo Emerson, "The American Scholar," in Brooks Atkinson, ed., *The Selected Writings of Ralph Waldo Emerson* (New York: The Modern Library, 1940), p. 48 (Phi Beta Kappa address delivered at Harvard University in 1837).

2. The present work presumes the French–English term *genre* to be synonymous with the German term *Gattung* and understands that they may be used interchangeably. For the most part, however, the former will be employed. A discussion of what is meant by the two terms appears below, pp. 24ff.

3. C. W. Votaw, "The Gospels and Contemporary Biographies," *AJT* 19 (1915): 47–73, 217–49; later published under the title *The Gospels and Contemporary Biographies in the Graeco–Roman World* (Philadelphia: Fortress Press, Facet Books, 1970). My references are to the Facet Books edition.

4. Ibid., pp. 1–2.

5. Ibid., pp. 2–5.

6. Ibid., p. 5. For views similar to those expressed above, see Martin Dibelius, *From Tradition to Gospel* (New York: Charles Scribner's Sons, 1934), p. 6; Rudolf Bultmann, *History of the Synoptic Tradition* (New York: Harper & Row, 1963), p. 369; W. D. Davies, *Christian Origins and Judaism* (Philadelphia: Westminster Press, 1962), pp. 12–13; Werner Georg Kümmel, *Introduction to the New Testament* (Nashville: Abingdon Press, 1975), p. 37; W. Marxsen, *Introduction to the New Testament* (Philadelphia: Fortress Press, 1968), p. 148; and Helmut H. Koester, "One Jesus and Four Primitive Gospels," *HTR* 2 (1968): 206, later reprinted in James M. Robinson and Helmut H. Koester, *Trajectories through Early Christianity* (Philadelphia: Fortress Press, 1971), pp. 158–204.

7. Votaw, "The Gospels," p. 5.

8. Ibid., p. 3.

9. Ibid. See also, for example, pp. 7, 11, 35–36.

10. Ibid., p. 11.

11. Ibid., p. 36.

12. K. L. Schmidt, "Die Stellung der Evangelien in der allgemeinen Literaturgeschichte, "*EUCHARISTERION: Studien zur Religion und Literatur*

des Alten und Neuen Testaments Hermann Gunkel zum 60 Geburtstag, ed. Hans Schmidt (Göttingen: Vandenhoeck & Ruprecht, 1923), pp. 50–134.

13. Ibid., pp. 84ff. See also pp. 90–114.

14. K. L. Schmidt, *Der Rahmen der Geschichte Jesu* (Berlin: Trowitzsch & Sohn, 1919).

15. Franz Overbeck, *Über die Anfänge der patristischen Literatur* (Darmstadt: Wissenschaftliche Buchgesellschaft, 1966), p. 23 (see also pp. 19–20). This work first appeared in *Historischen Zeitschrift* 48 (1882).

16. Dibelius, *From Tradition to Gospel,* p. 2. The words in parentheses were those employed in the original German version, Martin Dibelius, *Die Formgeschichte des Evangeliums* (Tübingen: J. C. B. Mohr, 1919), p. 2.

17. Ibid., p. 1.

18. Bultmann, *History of the Synoptic Gospels,* pp. 371–73.

19. For example, G. Bornkamm, "Evangelien, *synoptische,*" *Die Religion in Geschichte und Gegenwart,* dritte Auflage, vol. 3 (Tübingen: J. C. B. Mohr, 1958), col. 750.

20. Dibelius's concern appears in the English text of *From Tradition to Gospel,* where he refers directly to Schmidt's work (pp. 176–77).

21. W. D. Davies, *Invitation to the New Testament* (New York: Doubleday & Co., 1966), pp 115–16.

22. E. P. Sanders, *The Tendencies of the Synoptic Tradition* (Cambridge: The University Press, 1969), pp. 21–22; see also pp. 23–26.

23. William O. Walker, Jr., "The Identification on Compositional Grounds of Redactional Passages in Matthew," p. 4. This unpublished programmatic paper was presented to a Gospel Seminar on 21 September 1974, at Perkins School of Theology, Southern Methodist University. A revised version was published, "A Method for Identifying Redactional Passages in Matthew on Functional and Linguistic Grounds," *CBQ* 39 (1977): 76–93.

24. F. C. Grant, *The Gospels: Their Origins and Their Growth* (New York: Harper & Row, 1957), p. 28.

25. Lucian, *How to Write History,* vol. 6, LCL (Cambridge: Harvard University Press, 1959), pp. 10–17.

26. See Lucian, *How to Write History* 7; see also below, pp. 00ff.

27. This is also the conclusion reached by Charles Talbert, *What Is a Gospel?* (Philadelphia: Fortress Press, 1977), pp. 3–4.

28. A better procedure is to compare the gospels with various types of literature, regardless of what they may be called. Controls could then be applied in assessing the validity of the comparable features when such are identified. One would be more certain of reliable results from such comparisons in those cases where generic relationships were established.

29. See, for example, Hans Conzelmann, *The Theology of St. Luke* (New York: Harper & Row, 1960); Willi Marxsen, *Mark the Evangelist* (Nashville: Abingdon Press, 1969); and G. Bornkamm, G. Barth, and H. J. Held, *Tradition and Interpretation in Matthew* (Philadelphia: Westminster Press, 1963).

30. William G. Thompson, "An Historical Perspective in the Gospel of Matthew, *JBL* 93:2 (1974): 244, n. 2.

31. Consider, for example, the character of Arrian's *Discourses of Epictetus* which he explains in a letter to Gellius: "I have not composed these *Words of Epictetus* as one might be said to 'compose' books of this kind. . . . But

whatever I heard him say I used to write down, word for word, . . . endeavouring to preserve it as a memorial, for my own future use, of his way of thinking and the frankness of his speech. . . . This being their character, they have fallen, I know not how, without my will or knowledge, into the hands of men." Epictetus, *The Discourses as Reported by Arrian, the Manual, and Fragments,* LCL, vol. 1 (Cambridge: Harvard University Press, 1967), pp. 4–7.

32. An example of this dilemma is Jack Suggs, "Gospel, Genre," *Interpreters Dictionary of the Bible,* Supplementary Volume (Nashville: Abingdon Press, 1976), pp. 370–71.

33. Julius Schniewind, "Zur synoptiker—Exegese," *TR,* N.F. 2 (1930): 129–89.

34. James M. Robinson, *A New Quest of the Historical Jesus* (London: SCM Press, 1963), p. 55. See also, George A. Kennedy, *Classical Rhetoric and Its Christian and Secular Tradition from Ancient to Modern Times* (Chapel Hill: University of North Carolina Press, 1980), pp. 125–29.

35. Robinson, *A New Quest,* pp. 80, 89–90.

36. Koester, *Trajectories,* pp. 158ff.

37. Ibid., p. 162.

38. Ibid. Norman Petersen has offered a thorough critique of the kerygma–gospel hypothesis in a paper presented and circulated to the Task Force on Gospel Genre at the 1970 SBL meeting, "So-Called Gnostic Type Gospels and the Question of the Genre 'Gospel'" (The Task Force on Gospel Genre, 1970 SBL Gospels Seminar), pp. 11–17.

39. A discussion of James Robinson's theory of an evolving gospel genre is presented below, pp. 34ff.

40. Moses Hadas and Morton Smith, *Heroes and Gods* (New York: Harper & Row, 1965), p. 3.

41. Ibid.

42. Ibid.

43. Ibid., p. 17.

44. Ibid., pp. 17–18.

45. Ibid., p. 94.

46. For example, Morton Smith, "Prolegomena to a Discussion of Aretalogies, Divine Men, the Gospels and Jesus," *JBL* 90 (1971): 149–56.

47. Hadas and Smith, *Heroes and Gods,* p. 60.

48. Ibid., pp. 60–62.

49. Howard C. Kee, "Aretalogy and Gospel," *JBL* 92 (1973): 402–22; see also Howard C. Kee, *Jesus and History* (New York: Harcourt, Brace, Jovanovich, 1970), p. 122.

50. Hadas specifically identifies aretalogy as a species of biography (*Heroes and Gods,* pp. 3, 58). The emphasis upon the biographical character of the aretalogy is also reflected in the choice of the examples offered for consideration. More recently, others have affirmed a relationship with ancient biographical literature. See Dieter Georgi, "The Records of Jesus in the Light of Ancient Accounts of Revered Men," *SBL Proceedings* (1972): 527–542, and G. N. Stanton, *Jesus of Nazareth in New Testament Preaching* (Cambridge: The University Press, 1974), especially pp. 67–136.

51. Koester, *Trajectories,* pp. 187–93.

52. H.-D. Betz, "Jesus as Divine Man," *Jesus and the Historian* Festschrift

for E. C. Colwell, ed. F. Thomas Trotter (Philadelphia: Westminster Press, 1968), pp. 114–33.

53. Koester, *Trajectories*, pp. 187–88.

54. Ibid., pp. 189–90.

55. See, for example, Ludwig Bieler, *Theios Aner*, vols. 1 and 2 (Vienna: Buchhandlung Oskar Hofels, 1935–1936); and H.-D. Betz, *Lukian von Samosata und das Neue Testament, Texte und Untersuchungen*, vol. 76 (Berlin: Akademie–Verlag, 1961): 100–43; see also R. Reitzenstein, *Hellenistic Mystery Religions* (Pittsburgh: Pickwick Press, 1978).

56. David L. Tiede, *The Charismatic Figure as Miracle Worker* (Missoula, Mont.: Scholars Press, 1972), especially pp. 243–47. See also Carl H. Holladay, *Theios Aner in Hellenistic Judaism* (Missoula, Mont.: Scholars Press, 1977).

57. As far as I know, Robinson's use of the term *aretalogy* is independent of the work by Hadas and Smith.

58. James M. Robinson, "The Problem of History in Mark, Reconsidered," *USQR* 20 (1965): 136.

59. Ibid. See also Robinson and Koester, *Trajectories*, pp. 46–66, 266–68.

60. Robinson, "The Problem of History in Mark, Reconsidered," p. 136.

61. Ibid., p. 137. See also Robinson and Koester, *Trajectories*, pp. 46–66, 266–68.

62. Tiede, *The Charismatic Figure*, p. 1.

63. Ibid., pp. 253ff.

64. See note 27 above.

65. What is missing is a demonstration of those specific points at which the gospels as literary entities are comparable to other literary entities of antiquity. Only by clear demonstration of these points is one able to say that the gospels are examples of *bios* literature. One cannot move, as has Talbert, from myth to *bios* literature, without discussing those literary aspects which qualify the use of the word biography.

66. Consider, for example, Bultmann's statement related to the absence in the gospels of reference to Jesus' personality, appearance, character, origin, education, and development and the evidence of cultivated techniques of comparison (above, p. 8).

67. See above, pp. 6ff.

68. It is clear that the theological basis for the development and expansion of the mission of the church in Acts is derived from Luke's portrayal of Jesus in his gospel. Indeed, there are strong, convincing arguments for a type E classification under Talbert's system.

69. It is true that biographies of the ancient world were sometimes written in defense of a subject's character. Such attempts as, for example, Tacitus's *Agricola* were rarely covert, but, rather, clearly stated and developed. The gospels, on the other hand, give no overt testimony to such biographical motivation. Defense of character has, however, surfaced in the more recent analyses of those supposed opponents and their heresies to whom the gospels might have been addressed. Whereas the refinement and improvement of portraits is to be expected in treatments of subjects by different authors, dispelling false images is another, separate task, and one wonders if Talbert has not been unduly influenced by these more recent gospel "discoveries" in his description of category B.

CHAPTER 2—A GENRE FOR THE GOSPELS

1. William G. Doty, "The Concept of Genre in Literary Analysis," *SBL Proceedings* (1972), pp. 413–14.

2. Arnaldo Momigliano, *The Development of Greek Biography* (Cambridge: Harvard University Press, 1971), p. 11.

3. Rene Wellek and Austin Warren, *Theory of Literature* (New York: Harcourt, Brace, Jovanovich, 1949), p. 216.

4. Doty, "Genre," p. 422.

5. Wellek and Warren, *Theory*, p. 216. See also Talbert: "An author communicates not only through a system of shared conventions (a genre) but also through modifications of those conventions." Charles Talbert, *What Is a Gospel?* (Philadelphia: Fortress Press, 1977), p. 11.

6. Wellek and Warren, *Theory*, p. 224.

7. This is implied in the "development" of biography. See, for example, D. R. Stuart, *Epochs of Greek and Roman Biography* (Berkeley: University of California Press, 1928). For change within a genre, see Francis Cairns, *Generic Composition in Greek and Roman Poetry* (Edinburgh: University Press, 1972), pp. 98ff.

8. See below, pp. 48ff.

9. Wellek and Warren, *Theory*, p. 225.

10. Doty, "Genre," p. 427.

11. Willi Marxsen, *Introduction to the New Testament* (Philadelphia: Fortress Press, 1968), p. 125.

12. Rudolf Bultmann, *History of the Synoptic Tradition* (New York: Harper & Row, 1963), p. 371. See also p. 10 above.

13. Momigliano, *Development of Greek Biography*, p. 17.

14. G. N. Stanton, *Jesus of Nazareth in New Testament Preaching* (Cambridge: The University Press, 1974), pp. 118ff.

15. E. D. Hirsch, *Validity in Interpretation* (New Haven: Yale University Press, 1967), p. 104.

16. Wellek and Warren, *Theory*, p. 225.

17. Doty, "Genre," p. 428.

18. Ibid., p. 434.

19. Wellek and Warren, *Theory*, p. 221.

20. An example of the continued influence of this more limited understanding of "form" within the confines of genre criticism as applied to the gospels occurs in a book by J. Rohde, whose primary concern is with the merits and contributions of redaction criticism: "It was precisely by detaching this framework from the rest of the original traditional material that it became possible to see the framework itself as an entity *sui generis* and to interpret it as such." See J. Rohde, *Rediscovering the Teaching of the Evangelists* (Philadelphia: Westminster Press, 1968), p. 33. Another is Howard C. Kee's critique (cited above) against Hadas and Smith's aretalogical patterns, based on the fact that none of the examples offered by Smith portrays the death of a martyr. Genre, as a concept, transcends this strict understanding of form, an understanding which presupposed the absolute conformity by rote to the rules associated with a given genre. Unless there is a broadening of this sense of "form" in New Testament studies to include generic meaning—which, incidently, is

not at odds with early form critical theorists such as Gunkel—the separation of genre criticism from form criticism for the development and application of the former to the New Testament texts, especially the gospels, is an absolute necessity. In fact, the call for such separation has already been urged upon us by Petersen ("So-called Gnostic Type") and Doty ("Genre").

21. See above, p. 25.

22. Norman Petersen, "So-called Gnostic Type Gospels and the Question of the Genre 'Gospel'" (The Task Force on Gospel Genre, 1970 SBL Gospels Seminar), p. 25.

23. Ibid.

24. Petersen's argument specifically refers to the use of the term *gospel* as the genre title. This is not to be taken as an argument which denies the close relationships among the gospels, nor does it mean emphatically that there might not exist another classification into which all four gospels could be classified.

25. For example, James M. Robinson, "LOGOI SOPHON," *Trajectories Through Early Christianity* (Philadelphia: Fortress Press, 1971), pp. 71–113.

26. Petersen, "So-called Gnostic Type Gospels," p. 45.

27. Bernard Lonergan, *Method in Theology* (New York: Crossroad, 1972), p. 163.

28. See discussions in ibid.; Hirsch, *Validity*; Hans-Georg Gadamer, *Truth and Method* (New York: Crossroad, 1975); and Richard E. Palmer, *Hermeneutics* (Evanston: Northwestern University Press, 1969).

29. Petersen, "So-called Gnostic Type Gospels," p. 38.

30. Lonergan, *Method in Theology*, p. 159.

31. Roland Frye, "A Literary Perspective for the Criticism of the Gospels," *Jesus and Man's Hope*, vol. 2 (Pittsburgh: Pittsburgh Theological Seminary, 1971), pp. 206ff.

32. Polybius, *The Histories*, vol. 4, LCL (Cambridge: Harvard University Press, 1960), pp. 154–55.

33. Cicero, "To Lucius Lucceius," *Epistulae ad Familiares*, vol. 1, LCL (Cambridge: Harvard University Press, 1958), pp. 368–69.

34. Lucian, *How to Write History*, vol. 6, LCL (Cambridge: Harvard University Press, 1959), pp. 10–11.

35. Cornelius Nepos, *Pelopidas*, LCL (Cambridge: Harvard University Press, 1960), pp. 550–51.

36. Plutarch, *Alexander and Caesar, The Parallel Lives*, vol. 7, LCL (Cambridge: Harvard University Press, 1960), pp. 224–25.

37. Herein lies the difference between ancient *bioi/vitae* and contemporary biographies. To the modern mind, biography does not forfeit historical methodology in the development of the biographical treatise.

38. For a more detailed discussion of encomium and its importance in the delineation of the laudatory type of biography under discussion, see pp. 46ff.

39. D. L. Clark, *Rhetoric in Greco–Roman Education* (New York: Columbia University Press, 1957), p. 199.

40. Xenophon, *Scripta Minora*, vol. 7, LCL (Cambridge: Harvard University Press, 1956), pp. 60–61.

41. Isocrates, *Evagoras*, vol. 3, LCL (Cambridge: Harvard University Press, 1961), pp. 4–7.

42. Philo, *De vita Mosis,* vol. 6, LCL (Cambridge: Harvard University Press, 1966), pp. 276–79.

43. Lucian, *Demonax,* vol. 1, LCL (Cambridge: Harvard University Press, 1961), pp. 142–43.

44. Tacitus, *Agricola,* vol. 1, LCL (Cambridge: Harvard University Press, 1958), pp. 252–53.

45. See especially the works of Stuart, *Epochs of Greek and Roman Biography,* and Momigliano, *Development of Greek Biography.* See also Cairns, *Generic Composition,* p. 104, and Katherine Thaniel, "Quintilian and the *Progymnasmata,*" (Ph.D. diss., McMaster University, Hamilton, 1973), pp. 111–13.

46. It has been argued by Stuart and others that Greek biography descends from the encomium while Roman biography has its more immediate roots in the funeral oration (see Stuart, *Epochs of Greek and Roman Biography,* pp. 189ff.). Such a hypothesis does not, however, invalidate the present work. In the first place, by the time the gospels were written, Latin rhetoricians had incorporated the Greek encomium into their culture. Second, the gospels have close affinities with Greek tradition. Finally, the encomium and the funeral oration are both primarily concerned with the *topoi* and techniques of praise and are, in many respects, quite similar.

47. This term has been identified with a thesis of Gudeman in which he explains the genre of Tacitus's *Agricola.* Gudeman contends that the *Agricola* has been written· as a "biographical encomium" in accordance with the formal rules laid down by the rhetoricians. *Tacitus: Agricola and Germania,* with introduction and notes by Alfred Gudeman (Boston: Allyn and Bacon, 1900). See also R. M. Ogilvie and Sir Ian Richmond, "Introduction," *Cornelii Taciti, De Vita Agricolae* (Oxford: The Clarendon Press, 1967), pp. 12ff., and J. G. C. Anderson, "Introduction," *Cornelii Taciti, De Vita Agricolae,* ed. H. Furneaux, 2d rev. ed. (Oxford: The Clarendon Press, 1922), pp. xxivff.

48. Classical scholarship offers a parallel to our procedure which is worthy of note. J. G. C. Anderson has described a type of biography that was current and that provides the background for a proper understanding of *Agricola.* This biographical type is comparable to the type we have identified—indeed, the two appear to be identical. Anderson writes:

Biographies of this type were well known in Rome and familiar to Romans of Tacitus's day in the form of lives of political martyrs, such as those of Thrasea and Helvidius, to which reference is made in c. 2. They were all frankly eulogistic—encomia, not critical appreciations. The custom of writing them grew up side by side with, and perhaps directly out of, the practice of delivering funeral speeches . . . over the dead. They shared the purely laudatory character of these orations, and sometimes took their place. They were modelled either by direct imitation or indirectly, through influence of Greek rhetorical doctrine, on the Greek biographical encomium, of which the oldest surviving examples are the *Agesilaus* of Xenophon and the *Evagoras* of Isocrates. These two came to be regarded as models in this branch of literature, and formed the basis of the rules formulated by later rhetoricians for composition in the encomiastic style.

(Anderson, "Introduction," *Agricolae*, p. xxii. See the similar description by Ogilvie, "Introduction," *Agricolae*, pp. 11ff. Anderson's assessment is based upon the classic research of F. Leo, *Die griechisch–römische Biographie nach ihrer literarischen Form* (Leipzig: Teubner, 1901). At a later point in his discussion, Anderson argues against Gudeman's view that Tacitus's *Agricola* conforms directly to the formal rules laid down by the rhetoricians for the encomium. It is his conclusion which offers the precise parallel: "In short, so far as the *Agricola* conforms to the rhetorical rules, the correspondence is fully explained by the biographical nature of the rubrics which the rhetoricians drew up for formal encomium" (p. xxv). Thus, in effect, the argument is that the rules for the encomium actually mirror those characteristics commonly found in laudatory biographical treatises with which *Agricola* may be classified generically, and no theory of direct relationship need be posited. It is this "reflection in the mirror" to which our own investigation is directed.

49. Stuart, *Epochs of Greek and Roman Biography*, pp. 91ff.

50. Aristotle, *Rh.* I. 3. 3 and *Rh. Al.* 1421b. 5; Diogenes Laertius, *Lives of Eminent Philosophers* VII. 42; *Ad Herennium* I. 1. 2; and Quintilian, *Inst.* III. 4. See also Edward P. J. Corbett, *Classical Rhetoric* (New York: Oxford University Press, 1971), pp. 146ff.

51. *Philostratus and Eunapius*, LCL (Cambridge: Harvard University Press, 1961), p. xxvi.

52. See Diogenes Laertius, *Lives of Eminent Philosophers*, vol. 2, LCL (Cambridge: Harvard University Press, 1958), pp. 152–53. Also, compare the use of *demonstrativum* in *Rhetorica ad Herennium* with that of *laudationes* in Cicero and Quintilian.

53. See Quintilian, *Inst.* III. 4. 5. See also Corbett, *Classical Rhetoric*, pp. 146ff.

54. Aristotle, *Rhetorica ad Alexandrum*, vol. 16, LCL (Cambridge: Harvard University Press, 1957), pp. 316–17.

55. Quintilian, *Institutio oratoria*, vol. 1, LCL (Cambridge: Harvard University Press, 1922), pp. 396–97.

56. Aristotle, *Rhetorica ad Alexandrum*, LCL, pp. 304–05.

57. It is interesting to note (if only in passing) that other literary endeavors reflect similar methodological procedures. Recently, for example, William Farmer referred to the critical methodology of the Alexandrians which omitted passages from classical texts if and when such passages were considered to be "offensive to or unworthy of the gods." See William R. Farmer, *The Last Twelve Verses of Mark* (London: Cambridge University Press, 1974), p. 15. Citing evidence ranging from the fourth through the second centuries B.C. (evidence he feels to be relevant in certain respects to procedures adopted and utilized by early Christians such as Origen in the determinations of "accurate texts"), Farmer concludes that modification of classical Greek texts edited in Alexandria was "done with a conscious recognition of the fact that improved copies of the Greek classics were being made not so much to satisfy the curiosity of the antiquarians as to the practical needs of the contemporary reading public" (ibid.). Such text-critical practices would find close kinship with the technique of amplification under discussion, for they would include not only omission but also correction and even addition. One should note that such alterations were thought to improve the accuracy not to distort or falsify.

58. Isocrates, *Evagoras*, p. 2.

59. Stuart, *Epochs of Greek and Roman Biography*, p. 62.

60. Ibid., p. 77. Similar procedures are attributed to Theocritus by Cairns in his discussion of the *basilikos logos*. See his *Generic Composition*, pp. 110ff.

61. Stuart, *Epochs of Greek and Roman Biography*, p. 62. It is in such magnification that an author may display originality. So, according to Cairns, he may employ *macrolgia*, that is, "figures of thought" which are "simply means of amplifying upon, repeating, emphasizing, or magnifying a topos." See *Generic Composition*, pp. 119ff.

62. H. I. Marrou, *A History of Education in Antiquity* (New York: Sheed and Ward, 1956), pp. 272ff. Thaniel also identifies the encomium as one of the *progymnasmata* employed in Greco–Roman education ("Quintilian," pp. 94–114) and devotes a chapter to its function and influence as such. Cairns would further classify *progymnasmata* as a separate category of genres (*Generic Composition*, p. 75). As such, "they can be considered as the minimum formal rhetorical equipment of any literate person from the Hellenistic period on" (ibid.).

63. For example, Isocrates' *Evagoras* and perhaps even Tacitus's *Agricola*, although length alone tends to argue against delivery of either at the funeral. A later celebration, however, would have been an appropriate occasion for either work. See also Pericles' "Funeral Oration" (*Thucydides* 2, especially 41), and J. G. C. Anderson's comments (see above, note 48).

64. Thaniel devotes a chapter to a discussion of the encomium and the *topoi* employed therein. Clearly demonstrated is the influence of such *progymnasmata* on the literature of the ancient world. See Thaniel, "Quintilian," pp. 99ff.

65. D. L. Clark, *Rhetoric*, pp. 196–97.

66. Marrou, *Education in Antiquity*, pp. 272–73.

CHAPTER 3—GENRE EXAMPLES

1. Indeed, had the section on Theseus been preserved separately from the remainder of the encomium, scholars would perhaps smile slightly at a freshman's imaginative suggestion that the "Encomium of Theseus" might originally have been a part of another work in praise of Helen. While this is a speculative reading, it points to the problems created by Isocrates' digression within his larger work on Helen.

2. Birger Gerhardsson, *Memory and Manuscript* (Lund: C. W. K. Gleerup, 1961), p. 182.

3. See above, p. 50.

4. Arnaldo Momigliano, *The Development of Greek Biography* (Cambridge: Harvard University Press, 1971), p. 50.

5. D. R. Stuart, *Epochs of Greek and Roman Biography* (Berkeley: University of California Press, 1928), p. 69.

6. Momigliano, *Development of Greek Biography*, p. 51.

7. See above, p. 16.

8. Philo, *De vita Mosis*, vol. 6, LCL (Cambridge: Harvard University Press, 1966), p. xv.

9. E. R. Goodenough, *An Introduction to Philo Judaeus* (Oxford: Basil Blackwell, 1962), p. 147; see especially pp. 33ff., 145ff.

10. Philo, *De vita Mosis*, vol. 6, LCL, p. xiii. Goodenough acknowledges the distinctive features of *De vita Mosis*, but his discussion of allegory reminds us that Philo's methodology has not receded far into the background.

11. Ibid., p. xvii.

12. David L. Tiede, *The Charismatic Figure as Miracle Worker* (Missoula, Mont.: Scholars Press, 1972), p. 127. Cartlidge and Dungan also refer to Philo's *De vita Mosis* as an encomium and include this work under the section, "Greek and Jewish 'Gospels.'" Also included in this section are *Apollonios of Tyana, Poimandres*, and the satire "Life of Alexander," by Lucian of Samosata. David R. Cartlidge and David L. Dungan, *Documents for the Study of the Gospels* (Philadelphia: Fortress Press, 1980), pp. 203ff.

13. Philo, *De vita Mosis*, vol. 6, LCL, p. xv.

14. See above, pp. 53–54.

15. According to E. R. Goodenough, more than emulation is intended by Philo's treatment of Moses. Goodenough writes, "the career of Moses is not so much like the career of one who, like Abraham and Jacob, had the experience of development which we may reproduce, but was the career of the saviour of men who, given to them as a special loan from God can lead them out of the world to the apprehension of God. For the mystic experience of men consists in 'going up to the aethereal heights with their reasonings, setting before them Moses, the type of existence beloved by God, to lead them on their way.' (Conf. 95)." (Goodenough, *Introduction to Philo Judaeus*, p. 147.)

16. For example, see the discussions of the issues involved in J. G. C. Anderson, "Introduction," *Cornelii Taciti, De Vita Agricolae*, ed. H. Furneaux, 2d rev. ed. (Oxford: The Clarendon Press, 1922), pp. xxiff. and R. M. Ogilvie and Sir Ian Richmond, "Introduction," *Cornelii Taciti, De Vita Agricolae* (Oxford: The Clarendon Press, 1967), pp. 11ff. (See also note 48, chap. 2 above.) A similar discussion appears in Tacitus, *Agricola*, LCL (Cambridge: Harvard University Press, 1958), pp. 152ff.

17. Tacitus, *Agricola*, LCL, pp. 152ff.

18. Ogilvie, "Introduction," *Agricolae*, pp. 11–12, 14, 20.

19. Ronald Syme, *Tacitus*, vol. 1 (Oxford: The Clarendon Press, 1958), pp. 23ff.

20. See above, p. 39.

21. J. Arthur Baird, "Genre Analysis as a Method of Historical Criticism," *SBL Proceedings* (1972): 387.

22. Momigliano, *Development of Greek Biography*, pp. 11ff. Here it is clear that Momigliano includes both biography and autobiography in his treatment of the development of Greek biography.

23. Josephus, *The Life*, vol. 1, LCL (Cambridge: Harvard University Press, 1966), pp. 4–5.

24. Ibid., p. xiv.

25. Cartlidge and Dungan, *Documents*, p. 205. Except where otherwise noted, translations are from Cartlidge and Dungan's translation.

26. Ibid., p. 209.

27. Ibid., p. 211.

28. Ibid., p. 234.

29. Philostratus, *The Life of Apollonius of Tyana*, vol. 2, LCL (Cambridge: Harvard University Press, 1960), pp. 146–47. The emphasis is mine.

30. Cartlidge and Dungan, *Documents*, p. 235.

31. The use of "laudatory" is not inappropriate, since it conveys its histor-ical roots in the Roman rhetorical schools (see note 52, chap. 2, above). Since, however, our research includes the search for historically accurate terminology as well as descriptive terminology, the use of "encomium" more accurately conveys the Greek heritage.

32. We must acknowledge that whichever format was adopted, it was the "finished product" which received attention. As Stuart writes: "The ancient biographer was . . . chiefly interested in the man as he was when he had emerged a finished product. The chronicler tended to see in character and personality static things that it was his task to analyze and describe, . . ." (Stuart, *Epochs of Greek and Roman Biography*, p. 178).

33. A similar motive is evident in the autobiographical traditions attributed to an aristocracy in Rome (ca. 1 B.C.) which was interested in both the preservation of nationalistic ideals and an illustrious family heritage. See Momigliano, *Development of Greek Biography*, pp. 95ff., 103.

CHAPTER 4—THE RELATIONSHIP OF THE GOSPELS TO THE ENCOMIUM GENRE

1. Henry Fielding, *Joseph Andrews and Shamela*, ed. Martin C. Battestin (Boston: Houghton Mifflin Company, 1961), p. 13. *Joseph Andrews* was first published in 1742.

2. See above, pp. 2ff. and 6ff.

3. G. N. Stanton, *Jesus of Nazareth in New Testament Preaching* (Cambridge: The University Press, 1974), p. 117.

4. Ibid., p. 135.

5. David R. Cartlidge and David L. Dungan, *Documents for the Study of the Gospels* (Philadelphia: Fortress Press, 1980), p. 124.

6. B. P. Grenfell and A. S. Hunt, *The Oxyrhynchus Papyri*, vol. 11 (London: Oxford University Press, 1915), pp. 224–25.

7. Stanton, *Jesus of Nazareth*, p. 122.

8. Ibid.

9. Theodore J. Weeden, *Mark—Traditions in Conflict* (Philadelphia: Fortress Press, 1971), pp. 15–16. See also P. G. Walsh, *Livy: His Historical Aims and Methods* (London: Cambridge University Press, 1961), pp. 82–109.

10. See C. W. Votaw, "The Gospels and Contemporary Biographies," *AJT* 19 (1915): 1–2, as quoted above, p. 3; Roland Frye, "A Literary Perspective for the Criticism of the Gospels," *Jesus and Man's Hope*, vol. 2 (Pittsburgh: Pittsburgh Theological Seminary, 1971), above, p. 65; and Weeden, *Mark*, pp. 17ff.

11. Francis Cairns refers to genre identification in terms of primary and secondary elements in *Generic Composition in Greek and Roman Poetry* (Edinburgh: University Press, 1972), pp. 21ff. Using these categories, the primary element of the genre we have examined is the praise of the *bios,* and the secondary elements are the *topoi* and literary techniques required for the

fulfillment of the praiseworthy portrait. The presence of the primary element in the gospels will become apparent in the examination of authorial intent as well as in the discussions of the *topoi* and literary techniques (where that intent is also in evidence).

12. For example, compare Weeden's work on Mark and Talbert's on Luke–Acts (Talbert, Charles H., *Literary Patterns, Theological Themes and the Genre of Luke–Acts* [Missoula, Mont.: Scholars Press, 1974]). In addition, Talbert devotes one full chapter to John's gospel.

13. This is true because genre determination cannot be equated with the identification of a source or sources that have been utilized in the preparation of a given document. See above, pp. 30ff.

14. In this respect, it has been noted (accurately, I think) that the phrase *biblos geneseos* refers to more than just the genealogy which follows. For example, W. F. Albright and C. S. Mann write: "But for the first reader of Matthew, it called attention to the birth (*genesis*) not only of Jesus, but of the whole new order to which that birth gave rise." See *Matthew*, The Anchor Bible (Garden City: Doubleday and Co., 1971), p. 2, and Floyd V. Filson, *A Commentary on the Gospel According to St. Matthew*, Black's New Testament Commentaries (London: Adam and Charles Black, 1960), p. 52. The only qualification I would add to Albright and Mann's particular observation is that it is the beginning point of Matthew's presentation of the whole new order as initiated by Jesus whose story is about to be told. Further, the genealogy is midrashic in character and serves as an "interpretation and goal of history" designed to establish the predetermined character of the Messiah's coming. From its reading, one knows the Messiah has come. See Marshall Johnson, *The Purpose of the Biblical Genealogies* (Cambridge: The University Press, 1969), pp. 139ff.

15. Stendahl uses the phrase "holy irregularity." Krister Stendahl, "Matthew," *Peake's Commentary on the Bible*, ed. Matthew Black and H. H. Rowley (London: Thomas Nelson & Sons, 1962), 674d, p. 771.

16. D. L. Clark, *Rhetoric in Greco–Roman Education* (New York: Columbia University Press, 1957), p. 196.

17. Stendahl, "Matthew," 675, pp. 771–72.

18. The use of dreams has already been noted as an example of divine intervention which points to the excellent nature of the subject, a theme encountered in encomium literature. With regard to the theme of the star related to the birth, see Albright and Mann, *Matthew*, pp. 14–15:

> In the minds of the people at that time, it was inconceivable that the birth of an important personage should go unattended by a stellar harbinger, and such a star is reported to have greeted the birth of Mithridates (ca. 131–63 B.C.). A late Jewish legend ascribes such a star to the birth of Abraham. But for Judaism there was another consideration, and that was the prophetic oracle of Balaam (Num. xxiv 17). The promise is that of a "star coming from Jacob"; not only would this oracle be well known, but in circles which studied the prophets to find interpretations of the contemporary scene (such as the Essenes) such an oracle could not in the nature of the case have been without fulfilment. A messiah's advent *must* be hailed by a star. (The leader of the patriots in the second

Jewish War, A.D. 130–135, Bar Kosba, changed his resistance name, which probably meant "son of a young ram," to Bar Kokba, "son of a star." This is known from the recently published Muraba'at letters.)

In spite of the statement that a messiah's birth "must" be accompanied by a "stellar harbinger," Albright and Mann do note the absence of a reference of the "that-it-may-be-fulfilled" type related to the star's appearance. Thus, here Matthew appears to be accenting the marvelous event apart from the motive of fulfillment so common elsewhere in this chapter. This leads to the conclusion that Matthew is following a more specific, genre motivation rather than making a theological assertion.

19. For these motifs, see also Rudolf Bultmann, *History of the Synoptic Tradition* (New York: Harper & Row, 1963), pp. 292ff. See also note 20 below.

20. This theme is cited by Quintilian (*Inst.* III. 7. 5) as evidence of divine origin. We have encountered it previously in Isocrates' *Evagoras* (above, pp. 66–67); in Philo's *De vita Mosis*, derived from the sources at his disposal (above, p. 71); and, in a related manner, in Tacitus's *Agricola* (above, p. 76).

21. The procedure referred to is the practice of beginning with the birth account and continuing through early signs of greatness based upon excellences of early childhood and youth. Such accounts point beyond themselves, thereby making more convincing and intelligible the praiseworthy character of the adult, which is the primary concern.

22. Birger Gerhardsson, *The Testing of God's Son* (Lund: G. W. K. Gleerup, 1966), p. 79.

23. A more extensive treatment of this theme will be presented below in connection with Matthew's use of the technique of comparison, pp. 101ff.

24. In this respect, it explains the name, "Field of Blood" (v. 8). See Bultmann, *History of the Synoptic Tradition*, p. 272 and A. W. Argyle, *The Gospel According to Matthew* (Cambridge: The University Press, 1963), pp. 210–11.

25. The fulfillment passage to which this pericope refers is Zech. 11:12ff. See Albright and Mann, *Matthew*, pp. 340–41; and J. C. Fenton, *Saint Matthew* (Harmondsworth, Middlesex: Penguin Books, 1971), p. 431.

26. See above, p. 93 for the use of *dikaios* in connection with Joseph.

27. See, for example, the use of dreams in Matt. 1–2 (above pp. 93ff).

28. The structure of the verses would tend to represent absolute confirmation on the part of witnesses, both those biased in favor of the opposition and mere observers. For Matthew, this is conclusive evidence of the identity of Jesus, which he discussed progressively in Matt. 1–4:11 (see above, p. 95); for this identification, Jesus as Son of God, has obviously been questioned, since no "Son of God" could conceivably have died in such a humiliating manner.

29. Bultmann, *History of the Synoptic Tradition*, p. 306.

30. See above, pp. 80ff.

31. See above, pp. 69ff.

32. See above, pp. 39ff.

33. Perhaps examples of the type of argument to which we refer should be made more explicit. Take, for example, the following: Mark must have pre-

ceded Matthew, otherwise how can one account for the absence of so many of
the sayings' traditions from his narrative? Or, similarly, if Luke had had
Matthew before him, how is one to account for the obvious discrepancies
between Matthew's presentation of the Sermon on the Mount and Luke's
Sermon on the Plain (or the Lord's Prayer, for that matter)? There are several
fallacies in the above arguments, even though the logic implicit in them may
appear sound. For one thing, they presuppose that the precise intentions of
each author are known to us and we could therefore say that Mark (Matthew,
Luke, or John) would have functioned in a certain way if all the materials
were before him. For another, they presuppose a loyalty to a tradition which
may not, in fact, have been operative. In spite of the fact that loyalty to
tradition is apparent in the synoptics, it is certain that allegiance to traditions
was not always exercised in rote fashion apart from authorial intent. Also, the
tension between "author" and "copier" may be far more complex than most of
us are willing to admit. In any case, these arguments (and others like them)
must be considered highly suspect in view of the varying emphases evident
when one gospel is set alongside another. The answer to such arguments may
be as simple as this: what is omitted was not considered essential, for one
reason or another, to the particular portrait Mark (Matthew, Luke, or John)
was attempting to paint. Or, conversely, it may point to complexities which
are impossible for the historian to unravel. It is hoped that the answers to the
problems to which such arguments have been addressed lie somewhere in
between these polar positions.

34. The harmonizing of the opponents (and message) of Jesus with John is
not evident until one reads further in the gospel. Here, John is portrayed as
if on his own terms.

35. See also the prescriptions of Theon as presented by H. I. Marrou, *A
History of Education in Antiquity* (New York: Sheed and Ward, 1956), pp.
99ff.

CONCLUSION

1. Robert Henri, *The Art Spirit* (Philadelphia: J. B. Lippincott Company,
1923), p. 111.

Bibliography

I. TEXTS AND TRANSLATIONS

Aland, Kurt. *Synopsis Quattuor Evangeliorum*. Stuttgart: Würtembergische Bibelaustalt, 1964.

Aristotle. *The "Art" of Rhetoric*. Eng. trans. J. H. Freese. Vol. 22. Loeb Classical Library. Cambridge, Mass.: Harvard University Press, 1947.

――――. *Rhetorica ad Alexandrum*. Eng. trans. H. Rackham. Vol. 16. Loeb Classical Library. Cambridge, Mass.: Harvard University Press, 1957.

Cicero. *Epistulae ad Familiares*. Eng. trans. W. G. Williams. Vol. 25, Books I–VI. Loeb Classical Library. Cambridge, Mass.: Harvard University Press, 1958.

――――. *[Cicero] Rhetorica ad Herennium*. Eng. trans. Harry Caplan. Vol. I. Loeb Classical Library. Cambridge, Mass.: Harvard University Press, 1954.

Cornelius Nepos. Eng. trans. J. C. Rolfe. Loeb Classical Library. Cambridge, Mass.: Harvard University Press, 1960.

Epictetus. *Discourses*. Eng. trans. W. A. Oldfather. Vols. 1–2. Loeb Classical Library. Cambridge, Mass.: Harvard University Press, 1967.

Furneaux, H., ed. *Cornelii Taciti, De Vita Agricolae*. 2d ed., revised by J. G. C. Anderson. Oxford: The Clarendon Press, 1922.

Grenfell, B. P. and A. S. Hunt. *The Oxyrhyncus Papyri*. Vol. 11. London: Oxford University Press, 1915.

Isocrates. Eng. trans. of Vols. 1 and 2, George Norlin. Eng. trans. of Vol. 3, La Rue Van Hook. 3 Vols. Loeb Classical Library. Cambridge, Mass.: Harvard University Press, 1961.

Josephus. *The Life*. Eng. trans. H. St. J. Thackeray. Vol. 1. Loeb Classical Library. Cambridge, Mass.: Harvard University Press, 1966.

Lucian. Eng. trans. of Vol. 1, A. M. Harmon. Eng. trans. of Vol. 6, K. Kilburn. Vols. 1 and 6. Loeb Classical Library. Cambridge, Mass.: Harvard University Press, 1961 and 1959.

Nestle, Eberhard and Kurt Aland. *Novum Testamentum Graece*. 25th ed. Stuttgart: Würtembergische Bibelanstalt, 1963.

Ogilvie, R. M. and Ian Richmond. *Cornelii Taciti, De Vita Agricolae*. Oxford: The Clarendon Press, 1967.

Philo. *On Abraham—On Joseph—Moses*. Eng. trans. F. H. Colson. Vol. 6. Loeb Classical Library. Cambridge, Mass.: Harvard University Press, 1966.

124

Philostratus and Eunapius. Eng. trans. W. C. Wright. Loeb Classical Library. Cambridge, Mass.: Harvard University Press, 1961.

Plutarch. *The Parallel Lives.* Eng. trans. B. Perrin. Vols. 1–10. Loeb Classical Library. Cambridge, Mass.: Harvard University Press, 1960.

Polybius. *The Histories.* Eng. trans. W. R. Paton. Vol. 4. Loeb Classical Library. Cambridge, Mass.: Harvard University Press, 1960.

Quintilian. *Institutio oratoria.* Eng. trans. H. E. Butler. Vols. 1–4. Loeb Classical Library. Cambridge, Mass.: Harvard University Press, 1922.

Tacitus. *Agricola.* Eng. trans. M. Hutton, revised by H. M. Ogilvie. Loeb Classical Library. Cambridge, Mass.: Harvard University Press, 1958.

Xenophon. *Scripta Minora.* Eng. trans. E. C. Marchant. Vol. 7. Loeb Classical Library. Cambridge, Mass.: Harvard University Press, 1956.

II. GENERAL

Albright, W. F. and Mann, C. S. *Matthew.* The Anchor Bible. New York: Doubleday & Co., 1971.

Argyle, A. W. *The Gospel According to Matthew.* Cambridge: The University Press, 1963.

Baird, J. Arthur. "Genre Analysis as a Method of Historical Criticism." *SBL Proceedings,* 1972.

Bauer, W., Arndt, W. F., Gingrich, F. W., and Danker, F. *A Greek–English Lexicon of the New Testament.* 2d revised and augmented ed. Chicago: University of Chicago Press, 1979.

Betz, H.-D. "Jesus as Divine Man." *Jesus and the Historian.* Festschrift for E. C. Colwell. Ed. F. Thomas Trotter. Philadelphia: Westminster Press, 1968, pp. 114–33.

————. *Lukian von Samasata und das Neue Testament.* Texte und Untersuchungen. Vol. 76. Berlin: Akademie–Verlag, 1961.

Bieler, Ludwig. *Theios Anēr.* Vols. 1–2. Vienna: Buchhandlung Oskar Hofels, 1935–1936.

Blass, F. and Debrunner, A. *A Greek Grammar of the New Testament.* Eng. trans. R. W. Funk. Chicago: University of Chicago Press, 1962.

Bornkamm, Günther. "Evangelien, *synoptische.*" Dritte Auflage. *Die Religion in Geschichte und Gegenwart.* Vol. 3. Tübingen: J. C. B. Mohr, 1958.

————. *Jesus of Nazareth.* New York: Harper & Row, 1960.

Bornkamm, G., Barth, G., and Held, H. J. *Tradition and Interpretation in Matthew.* Philadelphia: Westminster Press, 1963.

Bultmann, Rudolf. *History of the Synoptic Tradition,* Eng. trans. John Marsh. New York: Harper & Row, 1963.

Cairns, Francis. *Generic Composition in Greek and Roman Poetry.* Edinburgh: The University Press, 1972.

Cartlidge, David R. and Dungan, David L. *Documents for the Study of the Gospels.* Philadelphia: Fortress Press, 1980.

Clark, D. L. *Rhetoric in Greco–Roman Education.* New York: Columbia University Press, 1957.

Conzelmann, Hans. *The Theology of St. Luke.* Eng. trans. Geoffrey Buswell. New York: Harper & Row, 1960.

Corbett, Edward P. J. *Classical Rhetoric.* New York: Oxford University Press, 1971.

Davies, W. D. *Christian Origins and Judaism.* Philadelphia: Westminster Press, 1962.

――――. *Invitation to the New Testament: A Guide to Its Main Witnesses.* New York: Doubleday & Co., 1966.

Dibelius, Martin. *Die Formgeschichte des Evangeliums.* Tübingen: J. C. B. Mohr, 1919.

――――. *From Tradition to Gospel.* New York: Charles Scribner's Sons, [1934].

Doty, William G. "The Concept of Genre in Literary Analysis." *SBL Proceedings,* 1972.

Farmer, William R. *The Last Twelve Verses of Mark.* London: Cambridge University Press, 1974.

――――. *The Synoptic Problem.* New York: Macmillan Company, 1964.

Fenton, J. C. "Inclusio and Chiasmus in Matthew." *Texte und Untersuchungen.* Vol. 1. Edited by W. Eltester and Erich Klostermann. Berlin: Akademie–Verlag, 1959.

――――. *Saint Matthew.* Harmondsworth, Middlesex: Penguin Books, 1971.

Filson, Floyd V. *A Commentary on the Gospel According to St. Matthew.* Black's New Testament Commentaries. London: Black, 1960.

Frye, Roland. "A Literary Perspective for the Criticism of the Gospels." *Jesus and Man's Hope.* Vol. 2 Pittsburgh Festival of the Gospels. Pittsburgh: Pittsburgh Theological Seminary, 1971.

Gadamer, Hans-Georg. *Truth and Method.* New York: Crossroad, 1975.

Gerhardsson, Birger. *Memory and Manuscript: Oral Tradition and Written Transmission in Rabbinic Judaism and Early Christianity.* Lund: C. W. K. Gleerup, 1961.

――――. *The Testing of God's Son.* Lund: G. W. K. Gleerup, 1966.

Goodenough, E. R. *An Introduction to Philo Judaeus.* Oxford: Basil Blackwell, 1962.

Grant, F. C. *The Gospels: Their Origin and Their Growth.* New York: Harper & Row, 1957.

Hadas, Moses and Smith, Morton. *Heroes and Gods: Spiritual Biographies in Antiquity.* New York: Harper & Row, 1965.

Hempfer, Klaus W. *Gattungstheorie.* Munich: Wilhelm Fink Verlag, 1973.

Hirsch, E. D. *Validity in Interpretation.* New Haven: Yale University Press, 1967.

Holladay, Carl H. *Theios Aner in Hellenistic Judaism: A Critique of the Use of This Category in New Testament Christology.* Missoula, Mont.: Scholars Press, 1977.

Johnson, Marshall. *The Purpose of the Biblical Genealogies.* Cambridge: The University Press, 1969.

Kähler, Martin. *The So-called Historical Jesus and the Historic, Biblical Jesus.* Eng. Trans. Carl E. Braaten. Philadelphia: Fortress Press, 1964.

Käsemann, Ernst. "The Problem of the Historical Jesus." *Essays on New Testament Themes.* Philadelphia: Fortress Press edition, 1982.

Kee, Howard. "Aretalogy and Gospel." *JBL* 92 (1973): 402–22.

──────. *Jesus and History: An Approach to the Study of the Gospels.* New York: Harcourt, Brace, Jovanovich, 1970.

Kennedy, George A. *Classical Rhetoric and Its Christian and Secular Tradition from Ancient to Modern Times.* Chapel Hill: University of North Carolina Press, 1980.

Koester, Helmut H. "One Jesus and Four Primitive Gospels." *HTR* 2 (1968): 203–47. Reprinted in Robinson, James and Koester, H. *Trajectories Through Early Christianity.* Philadelphia: Fortress Press, 1971, pp. 158–204.

Kümmel, Werner Georg. *Introduction to the New Testament.* Eng. trans. Howard Kee. Nashville: Abingdon Press, 1975.

Leo, F. *Die Griechisch-römische Biographie nach ihrer literarischen Form.* Leipzig: Teubner, 1901.

Lonergan, Bernard. *Method in Theology.* New York: Crossroad, 1972.

Marrou, H. I. *A History of Education in Antiquity.* New York: Sheed and Ward, 1956.

Marxsen, Willi. *Introduction to the New Testament.* Philadelphia: Fortress Press, 1968.

──────. *Mark the Evangelist: Studies on the Redaction History of the Gospel,* Eng. trans. Roy A. Harrisville et al. (Nashville: Abingdon Press, 1969).

Momigliano, Arnaldo. *The Development of Greek Biography.* Cambridge: Harvard University Press, 1971.

Moulton, W. F. and Geden, A. S. *A Concordance to the Greek Testament.* Edinburgh: T. & T. Clark, 1957.

Overbeck, Franz. *Über die Anfänge der patristischen Literatur.* Darmstadt: Wissenschaftliche Buchgesellschaft, 1966. (Reprinted from *Historischen Zeitschrift* 48 [1882]).

Palmer, Richard E. *Hermeneutics.* Evanston, Ill.: Northwestern University Press, 1969.

Petersen, Norman, Jr. "So-Called Gnostic Type Gospels and the Question of the Genre 'Gospel.' " (The Task Force on Gospel Genre, 1970 SBL Gospels Seminar), pp. 11–17.

Reitzenstein, R. *Hellenistic Mystery Religions: Their Basic Ideas and Significance.* Eng. trans. John E. Steel. Pittsburgh: Pickwick Press, 1978.

Robinson, James M. *A New Quest of the Historical Jesus.* London: SCM Press, 1962.

──────. *The Problem of History in Mark: And Other Marcan Studies.* Philadelphia: Fortress Press, 1982.

──────. "The Problem of History in Mark, Reconsidered." *USQR* 20 (1965): 131–48.

Robinson, James M. and Koester, H. *Trajectories Through Early Christianity.* Philadelphia: Fortress Press, 1971.

Rohde, Joachim. *Rediscovering the Teaching of the Evangelists.* Eng. trans. D. M. Barton. Philadelphia: Westminster Press, 1968.

Sanders, E. P. *The Tendencies of the Synoptic Tradition.* Cambridge: The University Press, 1969.

Schmidt, K. L. *Der Rahmen der Geschichte Jesu.* Berlin: Terowitzsch und Sohn, 1919.

————. "Die Stellung der Evangelien in der allgemeinen Literatur-geschichte." *EUCHARISTERION: Studien zur Religion und Literatur des Alten und Neuen Testaments Hermann Gunkel zum 60 Geburtstag.* Edited by Hans Schmidt. Göttingen: Vandenhoeck und Ruprecht, 1923. 2 Teil, 50–134.

Smith, Morton. "Prolegomena to a Discussion of Aretalogies, Divine Men, the Gospels and Jesus." *JBL* 90 (1971): 174–99.

Stanton, G. N. *Jesus of Nazareth in New Testament Preaching.* Cambridge: The University Press, 1974.

Stendahl, Krister. "Matthew." *Peake's Commentary on the Bible.* Edited by Matthew Black and H. H. Rowley. London: Thomas Nelson & Sons, 1962.

Strecker, Georg. "The Concept of History in Matthew." *JAAR* 35 (1967): 219–30.

————. *Der Weg der Gerechtigkeit.* Göttingen: Vandenhoeck und Ruprecht, 1962.

Stuart, D. R. *Epochs of Greek and Roman Biography.* Berkeley: University of California Press, 1928.

Suggs, Jack. "Gospel, Genre." *Interpreters Dictionary of the Bible.* Supplementary Volume. Nashville: Abingdon Press, 1976.

Syme, Ronald. *Tacitus.* Oxford: The Clarendon Press, 1958.

Talbert, Charles H. *Literary Patterns, Theological Themes and the Genre of Luke–Acts.* Missoula, Mont.: Scholars Press, 1974.

————. *What Is a Gospel?: The Genre of the Canonical Gospels.* Philadelphia: Fortress Press, 1977.

Thaniel, Katherine. "*Quintilian and the Progymnasmata.*" Ph.D. diss. McMaster University, Hamilton, 1973.

Thompson, William G. "An Historical Perspective in the Gospel of Matthew." *JBL* 93 (1974): 243–62.

Tiede, David L. *The Charismatic Figure as Miracle Worker.* Missoula, Mont.: Scholars Press, 1972.

Trilling, Wolfgang. *Das Wahre Israel.* Munich: Kösel–Verlag, 1964.

Votaw, C. W. "The Gospels and Contemporary Biographies." *AJT* 19 (1915): 47–73, 217–49. Later published as *The Gospels and Contemporary Biographies in the Greco-Roman World.* Philadelphia: Fortress Press, 1970.

Walker, William O., Jr. "The Identification on Compositional Grounds of Redactional Passages in Matthew." Paper presented to a Gospel Seminar on 21 September 1974, at Perkins School of Theology, Southern Methodist University. Revised as "A Method for Identifying Redactional Passages in Matthew on Functional and Linguistic Grounds." *CBQ* 39 (1977): 76–93.

Walsh, P. G. *Livy: His Historical Aims and Methods.* London: Cambridge University Press, 1961.

Weeden, Theodore J. *Mark—Traditions in Conflict.* Philadelphia: Fortress Press, 1971.

Wellek, Rene and Warren, Austin. *Theory of Literature.* New York: Harcourt, Brace, Jovanovich, 1949.

Wilder, Amos N. *Theology and Modern Literature.* Cambridge: Harvard University Press, 1958.

Wrede, William. *The Messianic Secret.* Eng. trans. J. C. G. Greig. Cambridge: James Clarke, 1971.

Index